Mindfulness for Law Students

Mindfulness for Law Students

Using the Power of Mindful Awareness
to Achieve Balance and Success
in Law School

Scott L. Rogers

Illustrations by Cathy Gibbs Thornton

Mindful Living Press
2009

Cover design: Cathy Gibbs Thornton

Library of Congress Control Number: 2009907260

ISBN: 0-9773455-1-3

For information about special law school discounts, send inquiries to contact@imslaw.com.

First Printing, May 2009

10 9 8 7 6 5 4 3 2

for Regina

for your encouragement and support,

and for a lifetime of inspiration and love

Table of Contents

Preface

The search for personal and professional balance has been a central challenge in my own life and career in the twenty years since I graduated from law school. At various times on this journey I have come closer to the ideal of balance, and at other times it has been quite elusive. In my work counseling law students, I aim to teach lessons about the importance of balance because I believe it to be a fundamental life skill that can lead to success during law school, and greater personal happiness and satisfaction in life beyond law school.

Scott Rogers has made a tremendous contribution to this learning in his book, *Mindfulness for Law Students*. The book innovatively weaves together many important techniques for integrating mindfulness into your daily life, with the philosophy and the science that underlie the importance of practicing mindfulness. While others have written on the importance of mindfulness, Scott is the only one who has applied these lessons specifically to law students. His own experience as a lawyer gives him the unique gift of understanding the road that you are on, and the ways that you can blend these ancient wisdoms to transform your experience as a law student and lawyer.

Every law student should take time before the first day of school to read this book. In fact, I would recommend that you treat yourself to a day in a quiet place that you enjoy—whether it be the beach or a park or your backyard—to read the book and think about ways that you can incorporate mindfulness and balance into your life in the years ahead. During your personal retreat you can also reflect on your goals for your law school experience in the year ahead. For some, it is to get the best grades possible . . . but it may also be to find the time to start a new clinic to help an underserved population, or to manage to remain a good parent or friend while in law school. This time for personal reflection is essential to evaluate and evolve your goals, and ensure that you are making the most of the precious opportunities you have been given.

Each of us is constantly presented with difficult choices in our lives. When facing the stress of upcoming exams—or your first brief, or a job interview—will you make the time to breathe, meditate, and exercise, or will you stay up all night, overcome by anxiety? Will you be the person who finds time to spend Thanksgiving with your family, or the one who takes a shortcut that results in an honor code violation? Will you remember law school as a time when you never left the law library, or as one where you learned a new hobby or ran your first marathon? This book may not answer all of these questions, but it will open you to ways of being more centered so that you can make good choices—choices that will lead to better results in law school in the short term, and greater peace and happiness in the long term.

These are choices you will be facing for a long time. You may wish to keep *Mindfulness for Law Students* in a safe and special place so that you can refer to it often in the future. Reading this book is a gift that you can give to yourself. You may respond to it differently as you move through the journey of law school and law practice. Enjoy!

Janet E. Stearns
Dean of Students
University of Miami School of Law

Foreword

Law schools do many things well, one of which is to produce anxiety and stress in law students. My own suffering in law school began in the evening of the first day of classes when my roommate and I puzzled over the "holding" in a property case: "The limitation over is void for remoteness." We knew a meaning for "holding" and for each word in the sentence, but when we strung these meanings together, we could make no sense of the product. This was the first of many moments of confusion and apprehension, which, when combined with the pressure of competition, produced a great deal of misery.

In recent decades, research and common experience have demonstrated that such suffering is common among law students, and can often lead to depression and substance abuse. It also may interfere with performance and satisfaction in all realms of life. In my experience, and that of many others, one of the best ways to deal with such suffering—and to enhance satisfaction and performance—is through the practice of present-moment mindful awareness, or mindfulness, by which I mean paying attention, moment by moment and without judgment, to whatever passes through the sense organs or the mind. It helps us to focus on the present moment rather than being perpetually stuck in the past or the future. A person typically cultivates the capacity to be mindful by silent meditation, and then endeavors to bring that mindfulness into life's daily activities.

Since 1998, a good number of individuals and organizations have sponsored mindfulness training—sometimes for academic credit—for students at more than a dozen U.S. law schools. Other developments related to mindfulness for law students (and lawyers, judges, and other dispute-resolution professionals) have included retreats, workshops, training programs, and articles in law journals and the popular press. I noticed an extraordinary burst of activity at a recent Northwest Dispute Resolution Conference at the University of Washington in Seattle: five sessions dealt with mindfulness, or closely related subjects.

In this book, Scott Rogers—lawyer and teacher—adds an exceptionally creative approach to bringing mindfulness into the legal profession. The great gift of this book is that it provides a simple, engaging, and unique way into mindfulness—even for those who are not quite ready to commit to an extensive meditation practice. The *Jurisight* approach is distinctive in two ways: First, it asks the reader to use his hands as a pathway into the body, mind, and spirit. Second, it explains the practice and philosophy of mindfulness through the use of familiar legal terms. Rogers suggests, for instance, that we bring "due diligence" to our thoughts and that we "seek relief" from our own judgments. In the same way that law students learn legal terminology as the code to understanding law, through this book they can learn to view many of these same terms as pathways toward self-understanding. This wonderful book also provides clear explanations of the neuroscience associated with mindfulness.

Although I have been meditating for many years, and teaching mindfulness to law students, lawyers, mediators, and others since 1999, I have learned a great deal from Scott Rogers—and I think you will, too.

Leonard L. Riskin
Chesterfield Smith Professor of Law
University of Florida
Levin College of Law

Acknowledgments

The writing of this book is the culmination of two years' development of *Jurisight,*® a practical guide to understanding and incorporating mindfulness into everyday life. As such, it could never have been a solitary endeavor without compromising its real-world impact. I am grateful to the hundreds of law students and lawyers who have participated in *Mindfulness, Balance & The Lawyer's Brain, Worrier to Warrior,* and *Jurisight*® workshops and presentations, and with whom I have worked individually. The development of this program has been greatly influenced by the experiences, insights, and ideas you have shared and continue to share with me.

I am thankful to several law students—two of whom are now lawyers—for their enthusiastic embrace of *Jurisight,* and, in many cases, their willingness to review and comment on drafts of this manuscript. Thank you to Giselle Mamamma (University of Florida, Class of 2008), Jessica Shore (University of Miami, Class of 2009), Ty Eppsteiner and Rebecca Wintering (Florida State University, Class of 2010), and Dale Dobuler and Wendi Ribaudo (University of Miami, Class of 2011).

I am deeply grateful to Janet Stearns, dean of students at the University of Miami School of Law. The rubber met the road when *Jurisight* was offered to UM law students in the fall of 2008 as a six-week course. The process demonstrated yet another instance of UM's commitment to its student body. It also fostered ongoing student relationships that have allowed for an in-depth follow-up of the application of the principles and exercises taught. Thank you to Iris Morera for overseeing the program with such enthusiasm.

It was many years ago, before *Jurisight* took robust form, that my dear friend, Mel Rubin, invited me to speak on mindfulness to his mediation class at the University of Miami. These first presentations formed the bedrock for what has followed. Thanks also to Bill Blatt for listening to me run through the entire *Mindfulness, Balance & The Lawyer's Brain* program one afternoon, offering feedback, and for inviting me to share this material with his law students. I am indebted to Jan Jacobowitz, director of UM's Ethics and Professional Responsibility Program, for sharing gems of insight that can be found in the Ethics and Professionalism chapter.

A movement is pulsing at the heart of this work—to bring contemplative practices to the everyday life of law students and lawyers. To my friends and colleagues at the Center for Contemplative Mind in Society, I thank you for the work many of you began before I opened my first casebook as a 1L student, and for welcoming me into your ever-expanding community. I am especially thankful to Charlie Halpern for bringing it all together, and to Douglas Chermak, Erica Ariel Fox, Stephanie West Allen, Gary Friedman, Rhonda Magee, Judi Cohen, Norman Fischer, Patton Hyman, Grove Burnett, Bob Zeglovitch, Ron Greenberg, Michael Zimmerman, Mary Mocine, Dennis Warren, Doug Codiga, Deborah Calloway, Daniel Bowling, Susan Jordan, Jack Himmelstein, and Clark Freshman for the many memorable conversations that have made a difference in the development of this material.

I also acknowledge my gratitude to my first teacher, Fred Eppsteiner, whose compassion and wisdom penetrates more deeply with each passing moment. I will also be forever grateful to Marty Peters, Professor of Legal Education at Elon University School of Law, who sparked my interest in formal meditation while I was a law student at the University of Florida and she directed its Law Student Resource Program. This early exposure led to my personal exploration of mindfulness and to developing ways of making it more accessible to law students—an intention come full circle. While Marty's influence took root in the late 1980s at the University of Florida, today it is embodied in the extraordinary presence and work of Leonard Riskin, Chesterfield Smith Professor of Law at the University of Florida. Len's encouragement, feedback, and, most of all, friendship, continue to inspire and motivate me, and energize the ongoing development of *Jurisight*.

To Joshua Shore, Tammy Sifre, and Jeffrey Gordon, I am grateful to each of you for the important contributions you have made to the Institute for Mindfulness Studies, the development of *Jurisight* as a method of teaching mindfulness, and to the organization and structure of this book.

I have been blessed to work with Cathy Gibbs Thornton over the past two years, developing the illustrations for this book. Cathy takes my rough sketches and creates an image that has a depth and meaning I hadn't fully grasped. I am also deeply touched and indebted to her for her tireless work in developing and refining the design and layout of the book. Many thanks, also, to Melissa Hayes, for once again proving to be such an exceptional copyeditor.

Finally, without the encouragement and support of my family, Arvey, Susan, Regina, Stacey, and Shana, along with the patience and faith of my wife Pam, and our daughters, Millie and Rose, this book simply would never have been written.

Introduction

This book was written for you, the busy law student. It introduces you to *Jurisight*, the mindfulness-based program developed for law students. As you embark on your law school career or persevere through its intense and demanding process, you are probably struck by an interesting paradox: While law school is one of the most exciting endeavors you have ever experienced, it can also be intimidating and overwhelming. The question is not to which side you lean, but whether you can embrace both at the same time. *Mindfulness for Law Students* is designed to serve as a guide for this very purpose. *Jurisight* introduces fundamental mindfulness insights and exercises you will find helpful for dealing with stressful situations while maintaining focus and clarity. Cutting-edge neuroscience findings are discussed throughout the book to illuminate the crucial role mindfulness can play in influencing the activity of your brain, including its structure and function, and with it, your success in law school.

Many students enter law school with the mind-set of very capable undergraduates. But law school is not merely an extension of your undergraduate education; rather, it is both a testing ground and an incubator of your physical, emotional, and intellectual fortitude. The three years of your legal education constitute a critical period in your development as a lawyer. The question is—how will you fare? While the career path you have chosen can be extremely rewarding, it can also leave you feeling burned out and underappreciated, and end up compromising your personal life, health, and well-being. But if you approach law school with your eyes wide open, and cultivate and maintain awareness of your inner experience so that it can guide you through challenging times, you will thrive.

Mindfulness offers you the following insight: The difference between meeting and falling short of your potential rests in *how you relate* to the law school experience, and not the experience itself. It is more about you, *on the inside*, than it is about the events transpiring on the outside. It is not the intense workload, but whether you can remain excited about the subject matter rather than crumbling under its weight. It is not the intimidating exam schedule, but whether you can move through the semester embracing the learning process with optimism and courage rather than becoming overwhelmed and defeated. It is not how you compare with your peers, but whether you decide to embrace them as a community with a shared mission and set of ideals rather than as a group of ruthless competitors. And it is not about whether your professors will hold you out as a shining example or berate you in class for overlooking the obvious, but whether you can

1

appreciate them for transmitting the knowledge, tools, and skills that will help you in your metamorphosis from lay member of the public to lawyer.

Mindfulness practices teach you ways of seeing more clearly what arises in your mind and body so that you may be more present, better grounded, and more successful in meeting the challenges you face as a law student. The mindfulness insights to which you are about to be introduced offer you the opportunity to glimpse more deeply the nature of your mind and to learn exercises that will help you relate more effectively to the varied stresses of law school, while enhancing your focus and well-being.

Mindfulness has long played an important role in my life—as a law student, a lawyer, a husband, a parent, and a human being. In law school, and afterward, when I served as a judicial law clerk and then began practicing law with White & Case, mindfulness meditation was a source of tremendous support and insight, especially during the intellectually daunting and interpersonally challenging moments that fill such experiences. Whether it was feeling overwhelmed by a massive amount of work and seemingly insurmountable projects; being consumed with self-doubt and worry; or the surfacing of angry and self-righteous impulses during hostile adversarial (and not so adversarial) exchanges, mindful awareness allowed me to relate to these difficult moments without identifying too intently with them.

Over time, my perspective began to shift as I related differently to the metaphorical rainstorms that cloud over and sometimes flood the law school experience. I began to watch and observe the coming storms, with the rain, lightning, and thunder brewing *within me*, as opposed to above me. From this state of mind, the experience was transformed. There was an inner quiet, an opening up of time so that false urgencies subsided, and a spaciousness with which to evaluate and make decisions. The journey is a process, and while I was still caught by it from time to time, it wasn't so troublesome, and it didn't consume as much of my attention; the storm lifted sooner. As it did, I found myself observing—with interest and compassion—that which had previously left me drenched.

I graduated law school first in my class because, I believe, I learned to watch the storms and enjoy the show. I maintained a high level of appreciation for my professors and classmates. When I took things too seriously and became anxious, overly competitive, or overwhelmed, I glimpsed how my mind was becoming trapped, and navigated myself to a place of greater balance. As a result, I was less concerned with momentary fluctuations in my interpretation of my experience, and better able to stay the course, ultimately making me much more effective at school.

Over the course of many years I discussed mindfulness with other people. It seems most people intrinsically appreciate the nature of their mind, and its tendency to wander into past and future. But, while meditation was of interest to some, more often than not it proved difficult to integrate into an already busy life. A natural outgrowth of mindfulness practice is that awareness begins to arise spontaneously, transforming everyday experience in powerful ways. Realizing first hand how mindfulness transformed these everyday moments, I decided that I wanted to develop pragmatic ways of cultivating mindfulness outside of a traditional sitting practice. The neuroscience provided support for the belief that an intentional shift of awareness could be extremely valuable, both in changing the experience and in rewiring neuronal pathways to set in motion long-term benefits. Maybe it would even work backwards, leading to an interest in sitting meditation.

Jurisight, the mindfulness-based teaching method developed specifically for law students and lawyers, is the embodiment of this approach. The insights you gain from this book will flow out of you, not off of the pages. Each chapter begins with a one-page *Overview* and concludes with a *Daily Practice* page, which sets forth a real-life example, a practice tip, and an exercise. The heart of each chapter consists of a collection of *Jurisight* terms to illustrate mindfulness principles. A *Resources* page concludes each chapter, listing relevant books, articles, and websites.

The book's ten chapters explore the ancient practice of mindfulness, illuminated with cutting-edge neuroscience research. Easy-to-learn exercises enable you to begin applying this material immediately. As the chapters progress, you will learn a series of related and evolving methods of cultivating mindfulness while in the midst of challenge. You will also learn basic instruction in sitting meditation.

You are invited to visit *The Mindful Law Student* website, which is found at www.themindfullawstudent.com, and where you can sign up to receive the law student newsletter. The website also contains demonstrations of all of the exercises presented in this book.

I hope you find this material to be stimulating and accessible, enhancing the extraordinary opportunities for personal growth and professional development afforded by your law school education.

> Scott L. Rogers
> May 2009
> Miami Beach, Florida

Mindfulness Made Legalese-y

This book was written just for you.

- There are many ways of learning mindfulness.
- There is only one method that was created specifically for law students.
- Jurisight for Law Students is that method.
- Jurisight uses legal terms and images to teach mindfulness.

This book is easy reading.

- This book is light on the eyes.
- This book is enlightening reading.
- This book may even make you chuckle.

LAW

This book is designed to help you to become a more effective law student and lawyer.

LIFE

This book is designed to help you to become a healthier and a happier person.

A Motion Practice

Almost all Jurisight® exercises involve the hands. Here's why.

- Your hands are always with you.
- With the hands as a recurring object of your attention, each exercise reinforces all other exercises, so you save time.
- Exercises that involve the hands activate the brain and connections to the hands take up a huge portion of your brain—so the exercises activate a lot of your brain.
- Great legal minds have always known that logic only goes so far. Jurisight exercises help you experience the present moment.

The life of the law has not been logic; it has been experience.
Justice Oliver W. Holmes Jr.

Jurisight® exercises are called *Learned Hand* exercises. Here's why.

- Learned Hand, one of America's greatest judges, was known for his mental clarity and insight into the law.
- The exercises are easy to learn. Easy to practice. Easy to apply.
- Your hands will begin to "wake you up" throughout the day to experience greater clarity of mind and insight into your life and the law.

Learned Hand **Exercises help you to redistribute your awareness throughout the day. You learn to press your own RESET button and establish a more balanced state of mind and body.**

Mindfulness Memos and Brain Briefs

Mindfulness Memos

- You'll read informative memos throughout this book that make mindfulness easier to understand and remember.
- The icon to the right will appear alongside Mindfulness Memos.

Mindfulness Memos are Mindfulness Cues

- Each time you see this icon, take a breath.
- Doing so, you will begin to catch your mind in distraction.

Brain Briefs

- At the bottom of most pages, Brain Briefs will update you on relevant neuroscience findings.
- The icon to the right will alert you to Brain Briefs.

Brain Briefs are Reminders of the Power of the Mind

- The Brain Brief icon is from the research of Harvard neuroscientist Sara Lazar, who found that mindfulness practices were associated with changes in the structure of the brain.
- The icon identifies the thickened cortical regions she detected in her groundbreaking research. We are grateful to Sara Lazar for use of the image.
- Sara Lazar used magnetic resonance imaging (MRI) to scan her subject's brains. You can learn more about MRI and other imaging technologies in the Glossary.

Mindfulness is something you can develop.
It can enhance your grades, your health, and your happiness.
That's what this book is all about.

CHAPTER 1

Mindfulness is an Intentional Act

This chapter introduces you to mindfulness. Mindfulness is all about cultivating awareness. Awareness of thoughts, feelings, and bodily sensations. Awareness of your life in the present moment.

At the outset, we will examine attention, distraction, and intention. In *Let the Buyer Be Aware*, the traditional role of paying attention to the breath is discussed, along with research exploring how mindfulness and paying attention can improve cognitive functioning and academic performance.

Tortuous Activity places a spotlight on the wandering nature of the mind and the role distraction plays in uprooting attention. The interplay of these two competing forces is something you probably can relate to on a daily, if not moment-to-moment, basis. Research is discussed that examines whether neurons in the brain respond differently to an object depending on whether it is the focus of attention or a distraction vying for attention.

In *Executing Your Will*, you learn that mindfulness involves paying attention to your intentions. The successful mindfulness program for dealing with obsessive thoughts is discussed as one example of how willful, mindful thought can change behavior and the brain's circuitry.

You will learn a basic breathing exercise that you can practice at any time to help you cultivate greater mindful awareness. It will deepen your ability to concentrate and focus with greater clarity at school and when studying for classes and exams. And it will help you to relax amid stressful events.

Let the Buyer Be Aware

Mindfulness is paying attention in a particular way: on purpose, in the present moment, nonjudgmentally.

Jon Kabat-Zinn

Mindfulness is Paying Attention

- When you choose to direct your awareness to an object, and sustain your attention on the object, you are practicing mindfulness.

- The objects of mindfulness practice include thoughts, feelings, and bodily sensations.

MINDFULNESS MEMO

The most popular mindfulness practice goes back thousands of years and is found all over the world. It involves resting awareness on the breath as the object of attention. When you realize your mind has wandered, you gently bring it back to the breath. This exercise steadies the mind, relaxes the body, and tones down mental chatter and distraction. There is a growing body of research supporting the powerful effects of this ancient practice.

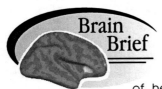

Brain Brief

At the University of Pennsylvania, neuroscientist Amishi Jah teaches a class on mindfulness meditation for students interested in finding balance and improving their academic standing. This class is offered as an offshoot of her scientific interest in studying mindfulness and cognitive functioning. Her scientific research with Michael Baime has demonstrated that mindfulness meditation improves a variety of cognitive and attention skills—and that even 30 minutes a day may improve the attention and focus of people with heavy time demands. At Hampton University, Pamela Hall looked at whether mindfulness meditation can improve grades. She found that college students introduced to an attention-focusing and relaxation exercise for a semester had significantly higher GPAs the following semester than a control group that had been matched for GPA but did not receive the mindfulness training.

Tortuous Activity

The faculty of voluntarily bringing back a wandering attention, over and over again, is the very root of judgment, character and will.

William James

The Distracted Mind

- It is the nature of the mind to become distracted and wander. You can train yourself to catch your wandering mind by practicing mindfulness.

- Each time your mind gets lost in the landscape of fear, worry, regret, and doubt, this experience is reinforced.

- Each time you catch your mind wandering on some tortuous path, you disrupt this discursive pattern of thinking, exercising your mindfulness muscle.

- As you practice mindfulness by catching your wandering mind, and returning awareness to the present moment, you bring balance to your mind and body.

MINDFULNESS MEMO

Mindfulness exercises can be practiced in a few seconds or over a longer period of time. They involve paying attention to something—like the breath, thoughts, the body, or emotions. The benefits that flow include stress reduction, focus, better immune functioning, and general happiness and optimism.

Brain Brief

Your life is filled with things competing for your attention. Assigned readings on the one hand, a social gathering on the other. How do you make your decision? And what influences whether you'll stick with it? Not surprisingly, the answer has a lot to do with where you *choose* to place your attention. When people's brains are scanned with fMRI machines while they are paying attention to one object (the "target") and ignoring another, neurons associated with the target fire more strongly than do neurons associated with the distraction. It is not so much the choices you have as it is how you choose to attend to them.

9

Executing Your Will

Leadership is the wise use of power. Power is the capacity to translate intention into reality and sustain it.

Warren G. Bennis

Become Your Own Beneficiary

- In the legal context, a person's will is executed by someone else after they die. But even when one is alive and well, they may not execute their own will.

- When you practice mindfulness, you execute your own will by paying attention to your intentions. You intend to do something, and you maintain your attention on this intention. This takes practice.

- As you will learn in Chapter Three, your brain responds in very positive ways as this deliberate execution of your will promotes neural integration, i.e., a more balanced brain.

- Attending to your intentions, you become the beneficiary of your own will.

MINDFULNESS MEMO

Mindfulness-Based Stress Reduction (MBSR) is an eight-week program for learning mindfulness skills. It began 30 years ago at the University of Massachusetts Medical School, and has been taught to tens of thousands of people. Its founder, Jon Kabat-Zinn, notes the importance of conscious intention—"the intention to practice, whether you feel like it or not on a particular day, whether it is convenient or not, with the determination of an athlete."

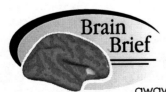

Brain Brief

UCLA neuroscientist Jeffrey Schwartz has been teaching mindfulness to people with obsessive compulsive disorder and relieving their symptoms. One part of his four-part method has patients "refocus" their attention away from an intrusive thought and toward the doing of an alternative behavior—e.g., from wanting to wash hands to gardening. To be effective, they must sustain this focus for about 15 minutes. PET scans reveal that this willful, mindful effort leads to a noticeable change in brain function and, ultimately, relief from their symptoms.

Daily Practice

Every moment of every day offers you the opportunity to wake up out of distraction and place your attention where you choose. As you are beginning to learn, each time you do this with intentionality, you become more proficient at it. Your attention is refined, your concentration enhanced, and you become expert at being present for your life as it unfolds.

Case in Point:

Julie had begun studying one evening, intent on finishing her Contracts outline. She had not yet gotten 10 minutes into it when she suddenly recollected how in college she would buy a Hershey's bar and eat one square each time she studied 15 minutes. This memory was laced with such a good feeling. The next thing she knew she was in her car looking for a store that sold Hershey's candy bars. "I never actually chose," she reflects. "This random thought and good feeling literally carried me away."

Exercise:

To investigate your attention skills and begin to work out your mindfulness muscle, set aside five minutes in the morning to practice Breath Awareness (see page 90). You will find this exercise challenging and relaxing. If you choose to do it for five minutes, set your intention on the doing of it. Part of the exercise is exploring whether you can meet your intent.

Daily Practice Tip:

When you find yourself getting agitated (for example, getting nervous, or angry, or feeling antsy), practice the above breathing exercise. You can experiment with the 4..7..8..10 variation on page 91, which you may prefer.

Resources

Books

Kabat-Zinn, J., *Wherever You Go, There You Are* (Hyperion, 1994).

Langer, E., *The Power of Mindful Learning* (Addison-Wesley, 1997).

Lewis, D., *Free Your Breath, Free Your Life* (Shambhala, 2004).

Schwartz, J., & Begley, S., *The Mind and the Brain: Neuroplasticity and the Power of Mental Force* (Harper Collins, 2002).

Articles

Allen, S., & Schwartz, J., "Law Students: Create a Well-Rounded Life," *The Complete Lawyer,* (2007).

Hall, P., "The Effect of Meditation on The Academic Performance of African American College Students," *Journal of Black Studies,* 29(3):408—415 (1999).

Jha, A., Krompinger, J., & Baime, M., "Mindfulness Training Modifies Subsystems of Attention," *Cognitive Affective & Behavioral Neuroscience,* 7:109—119 (2007).

Lutz, A, et al., "Attention Regulation and Monitoring in Meditation," *Trends in Cognitive Science,* 12(4) (2008).

Riskin, L.,"Awareness in Lawyering: A Primer on Paying Attention," in *The Affective Assistance of Counsel: Practicing Law as a Healing Profession* 447—71 (Marjorie Silver, ed., Carolina Academic Press, 2007).

Shapiro, S., Brown, K., & Astin, J., "Toward the Integration of Meditation into Higher Education: A Review of Research," Prepared for the Contemplative Mind in Society (October 2008).

Websites

Center for Mindfulness (UMass Medical School),
www.umassmed.edu/cfm

Adverse Judgments

In this chapter, you are invited to investigate the "judging" quality of your mind. At the outset, it is important to distinguish one type of judging from another—to distinguish King Solomon wisdom from the reactionary thoughts that continually arise in the mind and label events, information, and people as good and bad, right and wrong. The former is what we all strive for and is best termed "wisdom," while the latter unwittingly disserves our interests much of the time.

In the law, judgment is central. Judges judge. Jurors judge. And lawyers make judgments about the merits of their clients' cases and the efficacy of proffering certain arguments. It is important to develop the knowledge and the tools to be effective at making sound judgments. The law school experience is rooted in this enterprise. This book asks you to consider how mindfulness can prepare you to make better-informed and "wise" decisions.

Conflict of Interest raises the question of whether a great many of your thoughts might be biased and judgmental, independent of the facts. *Reserving Judgment* reminds you that not all judgmental expression needs to be given voice, and offers the mindfulness way of learning to observe judgments. *Relief from Judgment* builds on this and speaks to the benefits that flow from cultivating nonjudgmental awareness.

You will learn how becoming more mindful of judgments as they arise will help you gain greater mastery over your life—your ability to concentrate, your performance, the impressions you create, how you feel about yourself, and your general well-being.

Conflict of Interest

> *The ego makes a good servant but a terrible master.*
> ***Unknown***

Your Brain is a Judging Machine

- Just as the heart pumps blood, your brain pumps out thoughts.
- But, unlike your heart, which acts as a good servant, your brain is both servant and master. It generates thoughts and is their beneficiary.
- Like a judge ruling on her own case, many conflicts of interest arise.
- These conflicts lead to judgments—both self-serving and critical.

MINDFULNESS MEMO

One of the mind's most persistent activities is evaluating, categorizing, and judging. Good and bad, worthy and unworthy, safe and unsafe, happy and unhappy. It is as if all of experience is split in two, with one side regarded as right, the other wrong. While this tendency to judge everything has been adaptive for survival—good bear, bad bear—it rarely is applied for actual survival and often is counterproductive. Mindfulness invites you to learn to pay attention "without judgment." This process begins by learning to experience life with the bear that doesn't bite—"bare" awareness.

Brain Brief

Judgments are largely the activity of the prefrontal cortex. They are often preconceived, arising from cached content—fast and erroneous (quick to judgment). There can be little input from the sensory world. Mindfulness practices bring online "bare" awareness of the sensory world so that it may be more fully integrated into your experience and incorporated into your decision making. Real-time perceptions flow into the brain and mix with the preconceived. This integrated process is a more whole-bodied combination of intellect and experience, and, as such, is more genuine, and in touch with reality and the facts at hand.

Reserving Judgment

We should not pretend to understand the world only by the intellect.
The judgment of the intellect is only part of the truth.

Carl Gustav Jung

Learning to Pay Attention to Judgments

- Each time you recognize that your mind has entered a judgment, you have the opportunity to find relief from the arguments, miscommunications, and missed opportunities that otherwise would follow.

- As you become increasingly conscious of the arising of judgment, you can choose to experience the moment as an impartial witness by observing what is happening and allowing it to unfold.

MINDFULNESS MEMO

Practicing mindfulness, you become aware of "judgmental" thoughts and observe them arise and pass away. By not reacting so quickly, you come to appreciate that you have the choice of whether you will identify with the thought and act on it, proceeding down a familiar path, and neural pathway. Instead, you may practice allowing the thought to arise and being present for it. This insight frees you from habitual thinking, which can limit your potential in learning, relationships, and life.

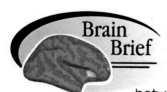

Brain Brief

Harvard neuroscientist Sara Lazar looked at the effects of long-term mindfulness meditation on the structure of the brain. Her subjects had been practicing mindfulness for an average of 40 minutes a day for between 2 and 16 years. Using MRI, she found regions associated with attention, interoception, and sensory processing were thicker in meditation participants than controls. These regions included the prefrontal cortex and right anterior insula. The degree of thickness correlated with length of time practicing mindfulness, suggesting that these changes in the brain developed with practice.

Relief from Judgment

On motion and just terms, the court may relieve a party . . . from a final judgment . . . for the following reasons; (5) the judgment has been satisfied, released, or discharged.

Fed. R. Civ. P. 60(b)(5). Grounds for Relief from Judgment

Finding Immunity

- Practicing mindfulness, you catch yourself criticizing and judging yourself and others. You begin to see how frequently these thoughts arise *sua sponte*.

- By observing judgments as activities of the mind, and allowing them to arise and pass away, they lose their mandate, and you are not compelled to execute them.

- Doing so, you find relief.

MINDFULNESS MEMO

Mindfulness practices do not seek to stop judgments from arising. Mindfulness practice is aimed at observing the judgmental thoughts that arise and watching them pass.

Mindfulness is about watching judgments arise with curiosity and interest. "Wow! That's interesting." Mindful awareness is nonjudgmental.

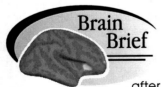

Brain Brief

Richard Davidson, of the Laboratory of Affective Neuroscience at the University of Wisconsin, and Jon Kabat-Zinn, measured brain electrical activity (EEG) before and immediately after, and then four months after an eight-week MBSR program. They found that the pattern of brain activation in subjects randomly assigned to practice mindfulness shifted significantly to the left-side anterior portion of their brains, a region associated with positive emotions. This shift in brain activation was correlated with a reduction in the amount of anxiety they reported.

Friendly Judgments: An Exercise

> *One cool judgment is worth a thousand hasty counsels. The thing to do is to supply light and not heat.*
>
> **Woodrow Wilson**

Judge Henry Friendly was, along with his predecessor on the Second Circuit Court of Appeals, Learned Hand, one of America's great jurists. One of Friendly's most salient attributes was that he did not have much of a judgmental bias one way or the other. He was free to respond in the moment to the facts and law before him.

This exercise invites you to meet the critical and judgmental thoughts arising in your mind with "friendly judgments." This means deliberately taking a stance that is less harsh and critical of yourself and others.

Instructions:

1. Notice when you are doubtful or critical of yourself or others. This could be in relation to school performance, eating, exercise, or general interpersonal style and effectiveness.

2. Pay attention to sensations arising in your body.

3. Bring awareness to your breathing, then to your hands.

4. Choose to respond differently, with compassion and patience.

5. Respond with thoughts, words, or deeds that are friendly and supportive.

6. Observe how this feels.

7. Observe how others respond.

Daily Practice

It can be tremendously beneficial to catch your "judging" mind in action. One reason is because the always-judging mind is rarely present, balanced, and at ease. The judging mind is searching for fault and mistakes. How often have you found yourself excited catching another's mistakes. You feel "satisfied" doing so. Your brain may even release pleasurable dopamine each time you do. What is not always realized is that often it is at the expense of someone else being told they are wrong. In the courtroom this is embraced. Among friends and at home, it may lead to unfulfilling relationships. Mindfulness practice offers an effective way to see the judging mind in action.

Case in Point:

David, a first-year law student, always saw himself as a happy, even-keeled guy. "Nothing bothered me too much. Everything tended to work out, so I had no complaints." After beginning to pay attention to his thoughts, David was surprised with what he found. "There was all this activity inside of me. It turns out I felt that people were letting me down all the time. As I saw this, I realized I was feeling disappointed and angry and it was affecting my relationships. The more I paid attention, the more I saw. It's a real eye-opener."

Exercises:

- To see your thoughts more clearly, practice Awareness of the Hands (see page 92). After a few minutes, wait for thoughts to appear. As they do, follow them, as if you were a private investigator, hired to see where they go.

- Read and rule on the Motion for Relief from Judgment found on page 106.

Daily Practice Tip:

- When you find yourself getting agitated (for example, getting nervous, or angry, or feeling antsy), turn what may appear negative into an opportunity to learn more about yourself. Take a breath and ask yourself, "What am I thinking right now that has me so agitated?" Take an interest in the answer. Note what it is, breathe, and move on.

Resources

Books

Doidge, N., *The Brain that Changes Itself: Stories of Personal Triumph from the Frontiers of Brain Science* (Penguin Books, 2006).

Elwark, A., *Stress Management for Lawyers* (Vorkell, 2007).

Halpern, C., *Making Waves and Riding the Currents: Activism and the Practice of Wisdom* (Berrett-Koehler, 2008).

Kabat-Zinn, J., *Coming to Our Senses* (Hyperion, 2005).

Siegel, D., *The Mindful Brain: Reflection and Attunement in the Cultivation of Well-Being* (Norton, 2006).

Tolle, E., *The Power of Now* (New World Library, 1999).

Articles

Allen, S., & Schwartz, J., "Exercise Mind Hygiene on a Daily Basis: Self-Awareness is the Key to Making Real Changes in Your Life," *The Complete Lawyer,* 4(3) (2008).

Davidson, R., Kabat-Zinn, J., et al., "Alterations in Brain and Immune Function Produced by Mindfulness Meditation," *Psychosomatic Medicine* 65:564—570 (2003).

Lazar, S., et al., "Meditation Experience is Associated with Increased Cortical Thickness," *NeuroReport,* 16: 1893—1897 (2005).

Websites

Mindful Awareness Research Center (MARC), www.marc.ucla.edu/

CHAPTER 3

The Neural Circuit Court

This chapter explores some of the exciting research in neuroscience, especially as it relates to learning, and to the relationship of mindfulness to the coherence of the brain's functioning. You may be surprised to learn that the structure and function of your brain is continually changing in response to your experience. This change is taking place even as you read these words and think the thoughts you think.

You will learn about three primary regions of your brain that are responsible for different types of functioning: the frontal cortex, the limbic system, and the brain stem.

You will spend a bit more time learning about the hippocampus, a horseshoe-shaped region located in the limbic area that plays an important role in memory and learning. You may be amazed to learn that new neurons can develop and take root in your brain and that the hippocampus is the site of some of this growth.

The hippocampus, you will also learn, is one of the sites in the brain that can be flooded with the stress hormone cortisol. You'll read what can happen if your relationship to stressful events leaves you overwhelmed or flooded.

You'll also learn about how practicing mindfulness may promote the integration of different regions in your brain, cultivating important traits for performance and well-being.

A Living, Breathing Constitution

The genius of the Constitution rests not in any static meaning it might have had in a world that is dead and gone, but in the adaptability of its great principles to cope with current problems and present needs.

Justice William Brennan

Neuroplasticity and the Changing Brain

- 200 years ago Thomas Jefferson, the father of our Constitution, had a limited view of its flexibility.
- 100 years ago Santiago Ramon y Cayal, the father of neuroscience, had a limited view of the flexibility of brain cells.

In the adult brain, nervous pathways are fixed and immutable; everything may die, nothing may be regenerated.

Santiago Ramon y Cayal

The Constitution on which our union rests shall be administered by me according to the safe and honest meaning contemplated by the plain understanding of the people of the United States, at the time of its adoption.

Thomas Jefferson

- The writing of Supreme Court Justice Brennan, quoted at the top of this page, represents a more modern view that the Constitution changes with the changing times and the American experience.
- As articulated by Harvard neurologist Alvaro Pascual-Leone, below, we now know that brain cells continue to be born and integrated into your neural circuitry. Synapses in the brain are continually forming and sloughing off as your brain undergoes constant change.

The brain is neither immutable nor static but is instead continuously remodeled by the lives we lead.

Alvaro Pascual-Leone

Gerrymandering

> *There is an ongoing competition for cortical real estate in the brain. [T]he first skills you develop get what you might call "squatter's rights" in cortical real estate.*
>
> **Norman Doidge, MD**

Neural Real Estate: Foreclosures, Rebuilding, and New Construction

- Until recently, scientists believed that neurons were hard-coded early in childhood and that their structure and function were fixed for life.

- This view has been replaced by one which recognizes the plastic nature of the brain, "neuroplasticity." Neurons grow and synapses change.

- Just as the legislature, the will of the people, can deliberately gerrymander voting districts, you can, through your will, deliberately reshape the structure and function of your brain.

MINDFULNESS MEMO

Your brain changes in response to your experience. It happens naturally, and explains why a violinist has a rich network of neurons associated with the hand that performs the fine finger movements. These neuroplastic changes are most robust when you choose to pay attention—and important changes to your brain are found even when you are engaging only your imagination. How you choose to experience your life, moment by moment, can change the structure and function of your brain.

Brain Brief

Harvard neurologist Alvaro Pascual-Leone had subjects play a five-finger piano scale for two hours a day for a week. Afterward, using transcranial magnetic stimulation (TMS), he looked at whether the size of the neural region associated with the finger movements used to play the scale changed. It did. The neural real estate had grown as more neurons were recruited to chip in. He had a second group of subjects *imagine* playing the piano scale for two hours a day for a week. Pascual-Leone found the same change—more acreage.

The Other Campus for Learning

> *There was this proliferative event occurring in the hippocampus that gave rise to new neurons.*
>
> **Fred H. Gage, PhD**

Don't forget the Hippocampus

- The hippocampus plays a crucial role in memory as it converts the contents of your "working memory" into long-term storage (e.g., studying for tests).

- Researchers have found the hippocampus to be a site of neurogenesis— the growth of new neurons.

- The hippocampus is located near the brain's emotional center, the amygdala. When you are stressed, the amygdala gets fired up, releasing cortisol which can impair hippocampal functioning.

MINDFULNESS MEMO

Mindfulness exercises that involve breathing and bringing awareness to the body can be helpful in toning down an overly engaged amygdala. As you practice breathing with mindful awareness, your prefrontal cortex becomes more effective at cooling down an inflamed amygdala and performing more optimally during consequential and challenging moments.

Brain Brief

Daniel Goleman writes about the neurobiology of "frazzle." As daily hassles unfold, the prefrontal cortex, home to your brain's executive functioning, is hijacked by the more primitive limbic system as too much of the stress hormone cortisol is released. As a result, attentional focus drops, along with the smooth functioning of the hippocampus and your capacity to learn. Working memory is diminished, mental creativity and flexibility are compromised, and there are fewer resources available to plan and organize. The importance of being able to maintain your cool is all the more important because the hippocampus is one of the places where science has confirmed neurons grow and proliferate.

A Split in the Circuits

[M]oral judgment is not a single thing; it's intuitive emotional responses and then cognitive responses that are duking it out.

Joshua Green, PhD

Your Brain: A Neural Circuit Court

- Your brain has 100 billion neurons, each connected to as many as 10,000 other neurons. There are three main regions of the brain.

- The *frontal cortex* is associated with higher cognitive functioning. The *limbic system*, especially the amygdala, is associated with emotions. The *brain stem* is associated with bodily regulation of breathing, body temperature, and the heartbeat. Brain fibers, many from the prefrontal cortex, connect these three regions so they can communicate.

- During times of extreme stress, these areas may not communicate so well. They may even inhibit one another's functioning.

MINDFULNESS MEMO

Mindfulness has been found to be associated with the following traits—attuned communication, body regulation of the flight or fight response, emotional balance, fear modulation, flexibility in response tactics, empathy, insight, and morality. These belong in a top-ten list for lawyering.

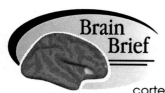

Brain Brief

UCLA psychiatrist Dan Siegel discusses how mindfulness practice activates middle-prefrontal regions in the brain just behind your eyes known as the orbitofrontal cortex, the medial and ventral regions of the prefrontal cortex, and the anterior cingulate cortices. Such activity engages fibers that link together disparate regions of the brain and body, strengthening connections among these regions and promoting "neural integration." When a professor is grilling you, your amygdala is firing "warning," and your prefrontal cortex is signaling "it's only a class." The more integrated your brain, the less you will experience a disruption or split in communication among the neural circuits.

Brain
Brief: Supplemental Brief

- **The runaway trolley.** Joshua Greene, a Harvard neuroscientist, studies the activity of neural circuits when people are making moral decisions. One study uses a classic philosophical thought puzzle involving a runaway trolley and the certain death of either one or five workers. In one scenario, subjects are told they can pull a switch diverting the trolley away from the five workers but, in doing so, kill another worker. Most people choose to save the five workers. In a second scenario, the five workers will be spared if a portly person watching the trolley from a bridge is pushed onto the tracks and killed. In this scenario, most people choose to not interfere, allowing the five to die. Philosophers have long puzzled over the reasons behind these different decisions.

In his research, Greene uses fMRI machines to scan the changes in blood flow in human brains in real time as subjects ponder these decisions. He finds that the first scenario activates the rational decision-making circuits found in the prefrontal cortex. The second scenario activates the brain's emotional processing centers; specifically, regions that interpret the thoughts and feelings of other people. When asked to explain their decisions, subjects have little insight into these processes. While these circuits are connected, the ways that questions are phrased or scenarios cast clearly engage some circuitry more than others. The degree of neural integration may well influence the communication of these circuits and the expression of a more balanced and wise decision.

Daily Practice

The power of imagination continues to surprise scientists. *Thinking does make it so.* As more is learned about the brain using scanning technologies, more is learned about the profound effect thoughts, and the inner world of imagination, have on the health and growth of the brain. Neuroplastic changes are connected with intentional mental activity, and mindfulness is one such activity. The information below will help you gain a "feel" for the plastic quality of your brain.

Case in Point:

Janine, a student in a workshop, was taken aback when she was asked to imagine signing her name. "When you asked us to sign with our dominant hands, I didn't think much of it. Then, when we did it imagining our other hand, I was struck by how much it was like real life. It was then I realized that it was real life. It was like my brain didn't know the difference. But I did. That was a strange realization."

Exercise:

• Select a musical instrument—preferably one you've played. Close your eyes and imagine yourself playing it. Hear the sounds and feel the instrument. Play soft and loud. Play slow and speed up until you're going as fast as you can. What do you observe?

Daily Practice Tip:

• At night, before you go to bed, take a moment and bring to mind one activity you'll be doing the following day for which a little rehearsal may be helpful. It may be studying in the library, paying attention in class, taking an exam, interviewing for a position, or participating in a school competition. Then, close your eyes and imagine yourself performing that task—choreograph the experience so that you are pleased with your performance—visualize, sense, and feel the experience. When you sleep, this mental rehearsal may well continue through the night.

Resources

Books

Begley, S., *Train Your Mind, Change Your Brain: How a New Science Reveals Our Extraordinary Potential To Transform Ourselves* (Ballantine Books, 2007).

Doidge, N., *The Brain that Changes Itself: Stories of Personal Triumph from the Frontiers of Brain Science* (Penguin Books, 2006).

Goleman, D., *Social Intelligence: The New Science of Human Relationships* (Bantam Books, 2007).

Medina, J., *Brain Rules* (Pear Books, 2008).

Siegel, D., *The Mindful Brain: Reflection and Attunement in the Cultivation of Well-Being* (Norton, 2006).

Articles

Allen, S. & Schwartz, J., "Law Firm Leadership on the Neuro Frontier," *Of Counsel* (2007).

Begley, S., "How Thinking Can Change the Brain," *Wall Street Journal* (January 19, 2007).

Rosen, J., "The Brain on the Stand," *New York Times* (March 11, 2007).

Websites

Brains on Purpose: Neuroscience and Conflict Resolution, www.brainsonpurpose.com

Lab for Affective Neuroscience, www.psyphz.psych.wisc.edu/

Mindfulness Elements

By now you have been introduced to the importance of attention to both mindfulness practices and concentrated study in school, and how mindfulness can enhance your attentional skills. You have been invited to look more closely at the judgmental and critical nature of much mental activity. Recent neuroscience findings highlight your brain's changing structure and function, and the role you play by actively choosing to attend to your experience—to be there for your life as it unfolds.

In this chapter, five Jurisight terms introduce you to fundamental mindfulness teachings. *Torture* examines the life cycle of a thought following an unpleasant event. Since events are always taking place and some of them will rub you the wrong way, it is helpful to explore the inner workings of your mind during these times. The four terms that follow offer a penetrating look into this dynamic. *Pain & Suffering* observes that people tend to distract themselves from painful experiences, which often leads to greater pain and emotional suffering. *Attractive Nuisance* explores how an unpleasant experience can start the mind wandering as thoughts form into judgments. Uninvestigated, these judgments are often accepted as true (*Hearsay*), and the mind locks onto them (*Attachment*) with even more thinking intended to help satisfy the judgment. This process can feel like torture, and limits your effectiveness in school, the level of fulfillment possible in your personal relationships, and your overall well-being.

As your attention and awareness of this quality of your mind develops, and you pay attention to your mind, you free yourself to optimize your potential for intellectual and social achievement and well-being.

Note: The Jurisight term *Torture* is not meant to be confused with humanity's history of inflicting unspeakable violence and pain on fellow human beings. The term is used to illustrate the powerful impact of a person's thoughts on their physical and emotional well-being, and draws on the language of classic writers such as Sartre, Krishnamurti, and even modern-day thinkers like Eckhart Tolle, who writes of the "daily torture" people inflict on themselves "by their minds."

Torture

> *Life does not consist mainly, or even largely, of facts and happenings. It consists mainly of the storm of thought that is forever flowing through one's head.*
>
> **Mark Twain**

Repetitve Stress Injuries

- Recall the ancient torture of water dripping on the forehead. While a drop of water may be mild, a never-ending drip can drive you crazy.

- Many of your everyday thoughts are judgmental chatter, involving criticism, worry, doubt, regret, and uncertainty. (Drip. Drip. Drip.)

- These thoughts can arise without awareness and slowly drive you crazy.

- Or, you can wake up and embrace them for the fertile insights they offer. Doing so literally changes your mind.

MINDFULNESS MEMO

Consider the life cycle of a thought. First, there is an event. For example, a professor increases your work-load prior to a test. Then, a thought about the event. Perhaps, "There's not going to be enough time to prepare!" Then a sensation, such as a queasy feeling, and feelings like frustration, worry, and anger. Soon enough, a reaction. Something like sulking, venting, confronting the teacher, or, perhaps, complaining to the administration. Of course, it all started with the event: more work. Just an event. Like a drop of water. Mindfulness offers this insight: It's not the event, *but your resistance to it* that sets in motion the discomfort and agitation. And consider this—your reaction often becomes someone else's event—your classmate's, your professor's, even your own. And unless someone is mindful of what's happening, you're likely to experience several rounds of thoughts, feelings, and reactions. The key is learning to see clearly your reactivity early enough to catch it and respond differently—more optimally, disrupting this conditioned pattern of reaction. See Illustration 4.1.

Brain Brief

Psychologists estimate that today you will have as many as 50,000 thoughts. That's a lot of thoughts—much of it mental chatter. A majority of these thoughts are repeats from yesterday, and the day before. They are the suffering that resists painful events. Think traffic, think relationships.

Conditioned Patterns of Reaction

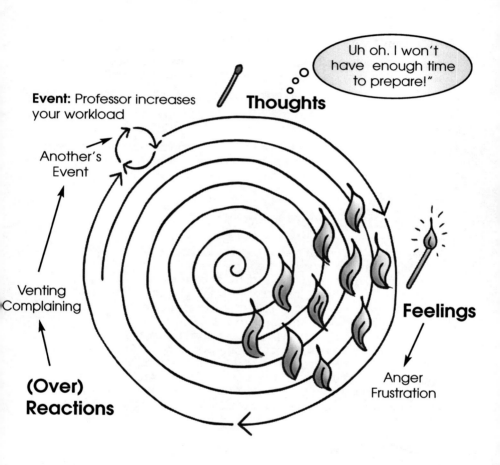

Illustration 4.1

Pain & Suffering

> *If you are distressed by anything external, the pain is not due to the thing itself but to your own estimate of it; and this you have the power to revoke at any moment.*
>
> **Marcus Aurelius**

Permission to Approach (the Pain)

- Life is filled with unpleasant events. In response to unpleasant events, a legal action may be filed claiming damages for "Pain and Suffering."

- Most people think the more pain a person feels, the greater their suffering.

- Mindfulness invites you to move into the pain and experience it directly by opening awareness to thoughts, feelings, and bodily sensations.

- Does this seem counterintuitive? Many report less pain and experience less suffering. They embrace the pain more fully and, as they do, the cascade of resistant thoughts and feelings (i.e., suffering) diminishes.

MINDFULNESS MEMO

When a person bangs their knee, a series of painful physical sensations arise. Often, people will react against the event in any of a number of ways: by complaining "Who left the cabinet open?" or worrying "Oh no! Now I might not be able to play in the game," or criticizing, "I'm so clumsy." The mindful way of relating to this painful event is to bring awareness to the breath and the sensations in the body. Mindfulness practices invite you to remain present and "be there" with the discomfort rather than distracting yourself from it. Such distraction results in a rash of thoughts and judgments "about the event." Mindful awareness brings you into direct experience with the event.

Brain Brief

When Mindfulness-Based Stress Reduction was begun 30 years ago at UMass Medical School, Jon Kabat-Zinn asked patients with pain to direct their "awareness" toward their painful bodily sensations. By bringing awareness to their bodies and the thoughts that were arising in reaction to the pain, these patients reported feeling less discomfort. Research has demonstrated similar findings with anxiety, depression, immune functioning, and sleep patterns.

Attractive Nuisance

> *I was trying to daydream but my mind kept wandering.*
>
> **Stephen Wright**

The Wandering Mind

- A focused mind performs optimally—studying, communicating, learning.

- The mind has a tendency to wander, following distractions and fantasies.

- When you daydream or get trapped in an uncomfortable series of thoughts, you often visit familiar places, going there again and again.

- Even though unpleasant, there can be something compelling about these places. They act like an *attractive nuisance*, drawing you in against your best interests.

MINDFULNESS MEMO

It's all about awareness. With awareness, you have choices. Without awareness, you stand little chance of not getting trapped in mental chatter and landing in a jail of your own construction. Look at the "Landscape of the Mind" illustration on the following page, and consider the places your mind wanders. The longer you hang out in the *River of Regret* or the *Valley of Fear*, for example, the more likely you are to become agitated and lose your edge. With awareness that your mind is in the habit of visiting *Attractive Nuisances*, you can catch it wandering earlier and earlier and bring it back to the present moment with greater mastery.

Brain Brief

Neural pathways in the brain have been likened to the trails on ski slopes. The grooves along the slope deepen as a path is taken again and again. Moreover, it is increasingly likely that a well-worn pathway will be taken the next time around. So, it's not that surprising when people repeatedly reenact the same painful thoughts and actions. But, you can choose to take a different trail, building and reinforcing a new pathway.

Illustration 4.2

35

Hearsay

> *It is the mark of an educated mind to be able to entertain a thought without accepting it.*
> **Aristotle**

Knowing When You're Out of Your Mind

- Hearsay is an "out of court" statement offered as evidence of the truth of the matter asserted.

- In Jurisight, Hearsay is an "out-of-the-mind" thought or statement believed to be the truth of the matter asserted.

- Many of today's 50,000 thoughts bear little resemblance to reality. Mindlessly, you believe them, unwittingly assuming the risk.

- Like legal hearsay, many of your thoughts are inherently unreliable and warrant further investigation before you allow them into evidence.*

MINDFULNESS MEMO

Of the tens of thousands of thoughts you think each day, many have little to do with what is actually taking place in the moments they arise. They are often triggered by resistance to the past and concerns for the future. In all likelihood, you experience them repeatedly. And you probably are so used to them that you identify with them, accepting many as true, and acting on them. With mindfulness practice, you investigate their reliability, as you would hearsay. Just as when you are successful having hearsay excluded from evidence, you can enjoy a similar feeling of elation when you have insight into your own hearsay and stop believing it to be the truth.

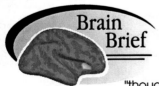
Brain Brief

Research into depression relapse has found the eight-week Mindfulness-Based Cognitive Therapy program to be as effective as medication or cognitive therapy. One of the key insights of this program, which applies to everyone, is that "thoughts are not facts." As you absorb this insight, your mind stops believing thoughts at face value—like "I am no good at this"—that historically have led to anxiety, anger, rumination, and depressed mood.

* One exception to hearsay is for statements regarding "then existing mental, emotional and physical conditions." In mindfulness, these are called *present moment experiences*.

Attachment

> *The great way is not difficult for those who have no preferences.*
>
> ***Dogen***

Satisfying a Judgment

- In the law, a writ of attachment is issued to satisfy a judgment.
- The mind is continually having judgments, based on preferences—likes and dislikes, hopes and fears.
- The mind attaches itself to what it likes and hopes will happen in an effort to satisfy the judgment.
- Given the uncertainty over outcomes and the inevitability of all things changing, attachments can be a source of unhappiness and suffering.

MINDFULNESS MEMO

As part of mindfulness practice, you learn to catch your mind as it attaches to wanting things or fearing outcomes. You realize that this is just your mind engaging in a conditioned ritual. As you observe your mind *with interest*, you witness the attachment and then the passing away of the need to attach. Doing so, you become less affected by distraction and torn with indecision. You free yourself to make better-informed decisions.

Brain Brief

In his high-tech laboratory, Richard Davidson, one of the world's preeminent neuroscientists, explores how attachment to an object may affect attention. A phenomenon known as the "attentional blink" occurs when a person is presented with a series of numbers and letters in rapid succession and asked to detect a specific number each time it is presented. When this target number is recognized, attention "blinks" as the same number, repeated about a half-second later, is overlooked. Davidson and his colleagues trained 17 subjects for three months in mindfulness meditation and found that none of them exhibited the "attentional blink." Even more, EEG indicated that their brain activity was less intense after detecting the initial target than it was for novices, freeing up more attentional resources.

Daily Practice

As you continue on your journey of "waking up!" and catching your mind as it wanders, it can be very helpful to bring your mind back to the object of your attention, prior to getting lost in distraction. Below are exercises you can practice that relate to each of the five Jurisight terms you learned in this chapter.

Daily Practice Tips:

- **Torture.** When you catch yourself (1) caught in thought, or (2) feeling agitated, or (3) overreacting, pause and reflect on whether you are caught in a Conditioned Pattern of Reaction (Illustration 4.1). Identify where you are on the spiral. Breathe.

- **Pain & Suffering.** The next time something or someone at school rubs you the wrong way, pause and bring awareness to your breathing. Approach your inner experience, allowing it to be just as it is.

- **Attractive Nuisance.** Study the *Landscape of the Mind* illustration and identify the places that are most familiar to you. Keep watch for the next time you visit one of these places. When you get stuck at one of them, observe yourself with interest and breathe.

- **Hearsay.** Listen to your peers when they are upset or frustrated, and note to yourself whether what they say is really and completely true. Turn this same lens inward when you find yourself frustrated. Ask a good friend to let you know if he or she hears you saying something that is an exaggeration. Be grateful to your friend, for this is often a thankless job.

- **Attachment.** The next time you are angry or upset, pause and explore whether you want someone or something to be different than it is. The next time you are very happy or elated, pause and consider whether you want something to stay just as it is. Reflect on how you would feel if what was "making" you happy changed, or what was "causing you" to feel distress did not change. This highlights the roots of attachment.

Exercise:

- Read and rule on the *Motion to Quash* found on page 109.

Resources

Books

Doidge, N., *The Brain That Changes Itself: Stories of Personal Triumph from the Frontiers of Brain Science* (Penguin Books, 2007).

Kabat-Zinn, J., *Full Catastrophe Living: Using the Wisdom of your Body and Mind to Face Stress, Pain and Illness* (Delta, 1990).

Williams, M., et al., *The Mindful Way Through Depression: Freeing Yourself from Chronic Unhappiness* (Guilford Press, 2007).

Articles

Blakeslee, S., "Study Suggests Meditation Can Help Train Attention," New York Times (May 8, 2007).

Kabat-Zinn, J., et al., "The Clinical Use of Mindfulness Meditation for the Self-Regulation of Chronic Pain." Journal of Behavioral Medicine, 8, 163—190 (1985).

Slagter, H., Lutz, A., et al., "Mental Training Affects Distribution of Limited Brain Resources." *PLUS Biology* (2007).

CHAPTER 5

Three-Tier Test for Finding Balance

You have been introduced to fundamental mindfulness teachings. You are acquainted with the benefits of attention and the challenges of a wandering mind (or is it the other way around?) You may see more clearly the endless arising of judgment in yourself, and begin to distinguish judgment that is grounded and balanced versus judgment that is reactive and defensive.

You appreciate the enormous number of thoughts that arise in the mind—how the mind attaches to these thoughts, and, believing them to be true, habitually implements their commands. You understand that the mind's tendency, when confronted with unpleasant events, is to distract and soothe by wandering into familiar places, even though they might be *poison pools*.

You have also practiced basic *Learned Hand* mind-body breathing exercises—methods for developing your attention skills, cultivating mind-body connection, and learning to observe the thoughts, feelings, and sensations that arise moment by moment.

All this leads up to the primary mindfulness insight: Embracing the thoughts, feelings, and bodily sensations that arise during such times offers a powerful method for finding relief and cultivating wisdom.

This chapter ties together these various insights and exercises, offering you a three-tier approach for finding balance amid moments of challenge and uncertainty. The primary *Learned Hand* exercise, known as *4—7—8 Hands,* constitutes the first tier. It integrates both breath and body and follows a *4—7—8* count. The breathing portion goes back hundreds of years and is helpful for anxiety and panic. Many lawyers and law students find the combination to be a source of relief during times of stress. You can apply it anytime you find yourself caught in a *Conditioned Pattern of Reaction*. It will help you find balance, toning down distraction and agitation, both as an end in itself, and so that you are better prepared to apply the second and third tiers, the *Due Diligence Inquiry* and *"Just Is" Awareness*. Together, they offer you insight and tools for disrupting habitual patterns of conditioning and for experiencing life in a more immediate and fulfilling way.

The Honorable Learned Hand

> *Breath is the bridge which connects life to consciousness, which unites your body to your thoughts.*
>
> **Thich Nhat Hanh**

- Breath awareness is practiced in many of the world's great spiritual traditions along with numerous meditative, medical, and therapeutic disciplines.

- The breath is a link to your involuntary nervous system, home of the flight or fight response, along with the relaxation response. It has a direct influence on moods and influences the whole nervous system.

- The average breath rate for adults is 12—15 breaths a minute. Practicing mindful breathing can lead to a slowing of this rate, which often is accompanied by physical, emotional, and mental benefits.

MINDFULNESS MEMO

Breathing is one of the only functions that is both involuntary and voluntary. While your very first breath may have been conscious, most of the breathing you have done since has been involuntary—it just happens. This is one of the reasons the breath is the most popular object of awareness. It also explains why it exerts such powerful influences on the body. As you practice the *Learned Hand* exercises, bring awareness to the breathing that happens, by observing it, and to the breathing you make happen, also by observing it. You will feel the effects immediately. *Let the breather be aware!*

Instruction for the 4—7—8 Hands exerise begins on the following page.

Brain Brief

Neuroscientist, Candace Pert, writes that bringing awareness to breathing can release peptide molecules from the hindbrain "to regulate breathing while uifying all systems." Andrew Weil advocates a 4,7,8 breathing exercise that forms the basis of the *4—7—8 Hands* exercise, to reduce stress, panic and blood pressure. Not to be taken lightly, breathing expert, Dennis Lewis cautions against practicing the breathing exercise more than a handful of times a day, especially if you have high blood pressure.

Tier One: 4–7–8 Hands

Practice this exercise both during times of calm and when in the midst of challenge. It takes about 15 seconds to do the exercise once. Find a time in the morning and evening to practice it, as this will help you call upon it with greater ease during moments of challenge.

To help you coordinate the movement of breath and the hands, separate instructions are given below so that you can practice each before putting them together.

The instruction below asks you to sit in a chair so that you can more easily learn the technique. In practice, you will find that you can do the exercise without sitting. Many are able to do it while standing and even when in the middle of interpersonal interactions. While you are keenly aware of what you are doing, it is unlikely that anyone will observe anything out of the ordinary.

Preliminary Instructions:

4–7–8 and the Breath
Inhale to the count of *four*. Hold your breath to the count of *seven*. Exhale to the count of *eight*.

4–7–8 and the Hands
Begin with your hands in a loose grip and fully extend your fingers to the count of *four*. Hold your fingers stretched open to the count of *seven*. Close your fingers, returning to a loose grip to the count of *eight*.

Instructions:

1. Sit in a chair—hands resting on your lap, each in a gentle grip.
2. Bring awareness to your hands and to your breathing.
3. Inhale and extend your fingers fully to the count of *four*.
4. Hold your breath and keep your fingers extended to the count of *seven*.
5. Exhale and close your hands to the count of *eight*.
6. Repeat this exercise two to four times.

Tip: If comfortable, inhale through your nose and exhale through your mouth, as if blowing through a straw. On the exhalation, place your tongue on the roof of your mouth just behind your front teeth.

You can use this exercise as a prelude to practicing awareness of the breath or of the hands.

Due Diligence

There are no whole truths. All truths are half-truths. It is trying to treat them as whole truths that plays the devil.

Alfred North Whitehead

The Truth, the Whole Truth, and Nothing But the Truth

- In the practice of law, prior to advising your client whether to enter into a deal, you conduct a due diligence inquiry to make sure that all representations made to your client are true.

- You can conduct your own due diligence inquiry to examine the truthfulness of the thoughts you tell yourself, especially when feeling overwhelmed, critical, frustrated, angry, sad, or anxious.

- This helpful inquiry begins by identifying a thought arising in your mind that may constitute suffering, and asking yourself, "Is this true?"

- If you find, as many do upon this simple reflection, that the thought may not be entirely true, you can free yourself from the pained state of mind.

MINDFULNESS MEMO

To be mindful is to be aware of what is taking place in your mind and body. Such awareness leads to ease of mind and heart. Often, due to stress, you can fall into reactivity where insight into present moment experience is curtailed. During such times—and you can feel them—it may be difficult to identify the thoughts that are arising in the present moment. Instead of identifying the thoughts, you identify *with* the thoughts. You can become flooded and overwhelmed by your mental or emotional experience. You become the emotion.

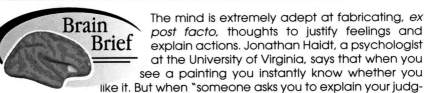

Brain Brief

The mind is extremely adept at fabricating, *ex post facto*, thoughts to justify feelings and explain actions. Jonathan Haidt, a psychologist at the University of Virginia, says that when you see a painting you instantly know whether you like it. But when "someone asks you to explain your judgment, you confabulate." Similarly, in moral decision-making, it is only after the emotions generate a decision that the rational circuits in the prefrontal cortex come online. Science writer Jonah Lehrer notes that "when it comes to making ethical decisions, human rationality isn't a scientist, it's a lawyer."

Tier Two: The Due Diligence Inquiry

You can conduct the Due Diligence Inquiry anytime, and usually very quickly. Insight and relief from momentary trappings of the mind often follow.

Sometimes it can be challenging to identify your thoughts. The questions which follow and the diagram on the next page will guide you through the Inquiry and provide a method for identifying obscured thoughts.

Remember, the Inquiry is as immediate and direct as asking yourself: **Is this true?**

▧ What is the Due Diligence Inquiry?
It is a simple question you ask yourself to see your mind more clearly.

▧ What is the question?
Is this true?

▧ What are the possible answers?
Yes and No.

▧ What if *it depends*?
Rephrase the question: Is this the truth, the whole truth, and nothing but the truth?

▧ Why do I want to do the Inquiry?
During the course of the day many thoughts surface in your mind that are reactions and judgments. Often you are unaware of them, or unaware that they are reactionary. Still, you accept them as true, which affects your language, conduct, and well-being. With these thoughts made explicit, the Inquiry can free you from this automaticity. You see through illusions, deceptions, and defenses.

▧ Where can I do it?
Anywhere. Anytime.

▧ How will I remember to do it?
At first you make a conscious decision. As you find relief, you will become more attuned to do so when you feel agitated. Over time, even subtle agitation will prompt the Inquiry, generating insight and relief.

When you become aware of agitation—for example, anger, frustration, guilt, worry, or sadness—make the decision to conduct the Inquiry.

Listen to what you are saying aloud or thinking to yourself. For example, "The professor's being totally unreasonable.!" If you are not able to articulate a thought, look to your emotions as a guide. Say to yourself, "I am feeling _**angry**_ (insert how you are feeling) because I think that _**the professor's being unreasonable**_." Often this will generate one or more thoughts you can then subject to the Due Diligence Inquiry.

STEP ONE

Inquire: *Is it true* . . . **that the professor's being totally unreasonable?**
Bring awareness to breathing, soften your gaze, unclench your jaw, drop your shoulders. Access your deep wisdom. Listen for an answer.

STEP TWO

If your answer is "no":	**Rest in awareness** of what you have realized. Know that you only see a piece of a much bigger picture.
If your answer is "yes":	**Ask yourself** "Am I sure?"
If your answer is still "yes" or "it depends":	**Rephrase the inquiry:** Is it the truth, the whole truth, and nothing but the truth?
If your answer changes to "no," you're not sure:	**Rest in awareness** of what you have realized. Know that you only see a piece of a much bigger picture.
If your answer remains "yes" or "it depends":	**Check in** to see if you feel any relief. If not, practice *4—7—8 Hands* or, proceed to the *"Just Is" Awareness* exercise on page 51.

Stare Decisis

> *Certainty is the mother of quiet and repose, and uncertainty the cause of variance and contentions.*
>
> **Sir Edward Coke**

The Paradox of Change

- *Stare decisis* means to "stand by the thing decided." It is a reminder that the law proceeds with caution and "with all deliberate speed."

- This quality is prospective—ensuring through precedent that the next legal moment is predictable. You may have been drawn to this quality, or, over time, it may rub off on you.

- Many are afraid and cautious of uncertainty and want things to stay just as they are. On the flip side, it is common to look to the imperfect past with regret and to want to change undesirable and unwanted events.

- This results in a paradox in which you want to change the past yet maintain the status quo into the future.

MINDFULNESS MEMO

The past can't be changed. The future can't be known. You appreciate this fundamental truth, yet still resist regretted (past), undesirable (now), and unwanted (future) events. Why? One reason is because they are a source of pain.

Uncomfortable with the pain, you distract yourself from feeling (facing) it. This short-term tactic can create unnecessary suffering. The desire to change an undesirable past or control an uncertain future rests in a mind that has expectations of the way things should be, and is frustrated when reality does not meet these expectations (see Illustration 5.1). This reinforces neural pathways that set these reactions into play in the first place.

Mindfulness offers an avenue to find relief by connecting with the deep truth that everything that has happened, is happening, and will happen, "just is." This insight transforms your relationship to the event as you allow things to be as they are—including unpleasant feelings—and sit with the discomfort. As you do, your relationship to the pain is transformed. You become readied to take action, grounded in the needs of the moment.

Paradox of Change

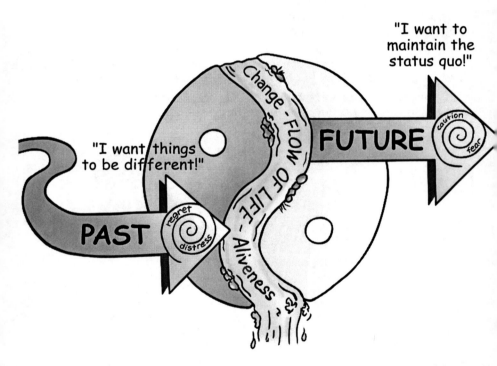

Illustration 5.1

Justice

> *For after all, the best thing one can do when it's raining is to let it rain.*
>
> **Henry Wadsworth Longfellow**

Finding Balance with What "Just Is"

- Justice is a noble pursuit that calls on wisdom, compassion, courage, and commitment.

- The pursuit of Justice is mindfulness in action. It draws on the present moment. You learn from the past, but do not resist it. You anticipate the future, but do not fear it.

- To ready yourself for Justice, you can cultivate a mind that embraces experience as it "Just Is."

MINDFULNESS MEMO

To be alive in the present moment is to embrace life fresh, with an open heart and an alert mind. There is no resistance to what arises, but rather a readiness for life's adventure into the next moment. This is a state of mind that can be cultivated through mindfulness practice. Embracing life as it "Just Is" is a liberating experience. You free yourself from the bonds of prior generations, your own conditioning, and everyone else's mind. This is the place from which your passions and gifts flow.

Brain Brief

The instruction to accept things as they are does not take a stance on what to do about the past, the present, or the future. Mindful acceptance is acknowledging what "just is." Participants in the various eight-week mindfulness-based programs, who practice observing the arising of ruminative thoughts about the past and fearful thoughts about the future, find relief. The research is persuasive that when these reactive thoughts and feelings are allowed to flow unimpeded by a resistant mind, melancholy and worry lessen their grip.

Brain Brief: Supplemental Brief

- **"There will be an answer . . . let it be."** The story of Wag Dodge and the Mann Gulch fire of 1949 is a lesson in the genius that flows from "Just Is" awareness. Dodge and his crew of 15 parachuted into the gulch to put out a small blaze. The winds shifted unexpectedly and the fire turned into an inferno, headed directly toward Dodge and his men. They retreated and fled—uphill. The fire, however, was moving too fast. There came a moment when Dodge realized it was futile to keep running. In that instant, he had an idea that would save his life. He was 30 seconds away from being burned alive when he thought to strike a match and light fire to the ground in front of him. Moments later he laid down in the burned ground, as the raging fire passed him by. He survived unscathed. Thirteen of his 15-member team perished.

Jonah Lehrer, author of "How We Decide," writes that once Dodge realized the "just is-ness" of the fire overtaking him, that his emotional circuitry, which up until that time had been caught in a panic and fueling his "flight," let go. When that happened, a part of his brain called the dorsolateral prefrontal cortex was liberated. Although no one had before done what Dodge was about to do, his brain's deliberative and creative processes accessed an array of associations and formulated his escape plan.

Tier Three: "Just Is" Awareness

"Just Is" awareness is a deep knowing that everything is as it should be. This can be difficult to comprehend, especially when things are not going the way you want them to go. But the two are not inconsistent. You can embrace events that are not as you wish them to be knowing that they are exactly as they are supposed to be . . . in the present moment. In his book, *The Seven Spiritual Laws of Success,* Deepak Chopra writes:

> *"Today I will accept people, situations, and events as they occur. This means I will know that this moment is as it should be, because the whole universe is as it should be."*

But this is easier said than done. You may even believe it to be true, but still that does not solve your problems or ease your discomfort. That is because "Just Is" awareness is deeply felt and known as wisdom. But when nothing more than a thought, "It just is," it can be as limiting as any other reactive thought.

The following exercises will help you connect more deeply to the wisdom of "Just Is." You can do them anywhere and anytime. They take all of a second, or as long as you would like to spend. Never underestimate the power of seeing the world as it "Just Is," even for a moment.

Two different exercises are set forth on the following two pages. The first, The Scales of "Just Is," is an active exercise that involves your hands and breathing.

The second, Noting What "Just Is," has two parts. They are less active and do not involve the hands.

They are meant to be separate practices, so do not try to do them one after the other. You may find that you prefer one more than the other. If so, practice the one that connects with you.

You can view a demonstration of these exercises on The Mindful Law Student website.

The Scales of "Just Is"

Practicing the Scales of "Just Is."

1. Place your palms facing up on your thighs.

2. Lift them a few inches and visualize yourself as a scale, with your hands as the balance pans.

3. Bring awareness to your breathing.

4. On an in-breath, visualize a weight landing in your left hand, lowering it while raising your right hand.

5. On an out-breath, return your hands to balance as the weight dissolves.

6. Repeat this movement of your breath and hands in and out of balance.

7. After repeating this cycle a few times, softly utter to yourself on the in-breath "Just" and on the out-breath "Is."

Doing so, you connect the breath, balance, and "Just Is."

This exercise is a reminder that *you are equipped to handle* all of the challenging events and situations that life brings your way.

Unpleasant events will occasionally throw you off balance. Using your breath and intuitive understanding of the "Just Is-ness" of life, you acknowledge that *you can bear what comes your way.*

In fact, you appreciate that *you were made for these times.*

Noting What "Just Is"

What "Just Is."

This exercise involves the nonjudgmental way of observing people, events, and experience. Practicing it helps you more easily shift into this mindfulness state.

1. Bring yourself into a comfortable sitting or standing position.
2. Bring awareness to your breathing.
3. Follow your breath for a few cycles as you move more deeply into a state of relaxation or focused awareness.
4. Look around with new eyes and note what "Just Is." For example, The table "Just Is." That man "Just Is." The sun "Just Is," and so on.
5. Do this for several minutes. Then, return to your breathing.
6. Close your eyes and listen with new ears and note what "Just Is." For example, The leaves swooshing "Just Is." The car honking "Just Is." The air conditioner running "Just Is," and so on.
7. Do this for several minutes. Then, return to your breathing.
8. During this exercise, try *not to think about* what falls into awareness. Soften your mind's grasping, and soak in the "Just-Isness" of your experience.

What "Just Is" Changing

This exercise is very much like the one above, but expands awareness to what "Just Is" *changing*. It is a reminder that while we tend to think of things as static and unchanging, and can be soothed by this belief, in fact, everything is constantly changing. The instructions below replace steps 4, 5, and 6 above.

4. Look around with new eyes and note what "Just Is" changing. For example, The wind "Just Is" shifting. That man "Just Is" growing old. The flower "Just Is" blooming. My heart "Just Is" beating, and so on.
5. Do this for several minutes. Then, return to your breathing.
6. Close your eyes and listen with new ears and note what "Just Is" changing.

Daily Practice

The 4—7—8 Hands, Due Diligence Inquiry and "Just Is" Awareness exercises are powerful mindfulness tools. Each time you apply one you will be disrupting old patterns of reactivity, laying down new neural pathways, and setting in motion a more effective way of relating to your life's experience. The trick is remembering to do so, or being willing to do so during times of challenge.

Case in Point:

■ Joanne is a third-year law student hopeful of landing a position in a tight market. She is bright, dynamic, and optimistic. Still, awaiting a key interview, she began to feel the familiar pangs of discomfort. This is what she had to say:

One thing stood between me and the law firm of my dreams—the interview. While I waited for the hiring partner in the conference room, I felt my heart beating out of my chest. Knowing how 4—7—8 Hands always calmed me down, I secretly did the exercise underneath the conference table. Instead of having an avalanche of worries on what could go wrong in the interview flood my mind, the Hands exercise kept me focused on my breathing as I waited. With the calm came confidence . . . and later that hour, a job offer.

■ Hector was convinced he blew the interview for a summer clerkship. *I kept saying to myself, "I blew it." I couldn't get it out of my mind. I was so angry at myself. Then I remembered Due Diligence. I asked myself if it was true that I blew it. In the stillness of that moment, I realized that I had no idea. How could I? And then, I felt this sense of calm. I said to myself, "You know . . . It Just Is. Everything will be okay." This really sunk in.*

Daily Practice:

• When you find yourself agitated or experiencing an afflicted emotion such as anger or fear, practice 4—7—8 Hands. Then conduct the Due Diligence Inquiry by (1) identifying a thought, and (2) asking if it is true. At other times, and it can be anytime, pause and observe the "Just Isness" of the moment.

Exercise:

• Read the Motion to Embrace Life's Uncertainties found on page 114.

Resources

Books

Brantley, J., *Calming Your Anxious Mind* (New Harbinger, 2003).

Chopra, D., *The Seven Spiritual Laws of Success* (New World Library, 1994).

Lehrer, J., *How We Decide* (Houghton Mifflin Harcourt, 2009).

Lewis, D., *Free Your Breath Free Your Life* (Shambdala, 2004).

Pert, C., *Molecules of Emotion* (Schribner, 1997).

Ricard, M., *Happiness* (Little Brown, 2006).

Rogers, S., *Mindfulness, Balance & The Lawyer's Brain* (Coursebook and 8 CD Set from Live Workshop, 2007).

Weil, A., *Breathing: The Master Key to Self-Healing, Sounds True* (Audio CD, February 8, 2000).

Articles

Allen, S., "Move from Being a Mindfulness Lawyer to a Mindful Lawyer." *The Complete Lawyer* (2008).

Rogers, S., "Experiencing Grade Anxiety: Mindfulness Offers Clarity," *Res Ipsa Loquitur*, 15 (UM Law School, February 2009).

Rogers, S., "Opinion: Managing Law School Stress," *Res Ipsa Loquitur*, 15 (UM Law School, March—April 2009).

Websites

The Mindful Law Student, www.themindfullawstudent.com

CHAPTER 6

Healthy, Wealthy & Wise

Now that you have a deeper insight into the workings of your mind, we turn to the connection between mind and body, and how mindful awareness can help you take good care of yourself.

As a law student, you have a great deal of work and may feel, from time to time, that things are overwhelming. This can create a lot of stress. In response to stress, the brain sends signals to the body to release cortisol. In moderation, this can be helpful, but when feelings of stress are intense or overwhelming, too much cortisol makes its way to the brain, inflaming the situation and compromising performance and health. This can affect your memory, inhibit your learning potential, and even destroy neurons.

Research has found that chronic stress can bring about headaches, irritability, lack of energy, sleep disorders, anger, anxiety, depression, and weaken your immune system. As you are beginning to learn, mindfulness practices can help you see more clearly what is taking place—both outside and inside—so that you are better able to respond to the small fires and little crises that flare up but usually don't amount to *clear and present* dangers.

In this chapter, you will be reminded of ways you can take care of yourself, focusing on your body. This includes exercise, eating, sleep, and the benefits of body-awareness, aromatherapy, and music. Neuroscience findings suggest how many of these approaches actually enhance your learning potential and overall productivity. Mindful that your brain is always changing in response to your experience, you can appreciate the extraordinary changes you bring to your work and life by developing a more attuned and reflective method of relating to your moment-to-moment experiences.

The Body of Law & Your Constitution

[The Constitution is] intended to endure for ages to come, and consequently, to be adapted to the various crises of human affairs.

Chief Justice John Marshall

Stress on the Body

- The body of American law continues to grow and the U.S. Constitution is continually challenged.

- You too have a body and a constitution—living and breathing. The law is continually tested and stressed. So are you.

- Mindfulness is a reminder to be deeply aware of and to protect and defend your body and constitution.

MINDFULNESS MEMO

Knowledge about health and your body is only as helpful as your intention to protect and defend it—with your life. As a law student, you spend a great deal of time in your head—in a very real sense (or non-sense), removed from your body. Mindfulness practices help keep you connected to the important signals your body sends you throughout the day. When stressed, your adrenal glands release a hormone called cortisol—which can be really helpful if you're being chased by a bear to get you going. When you're being chased by a worrisome thought, it can be destructive as it inflames your amygdala, the brain's emotional center. This can lead to emotional flooding as surging cortisol impairs the functioning of your prefrontal cortex, which is trying to tell you that "there is no bear!" All this can happen when you're sitting in class, thinking about an exam, awaiting an interview, taking an exam, waking up at 3:00 in the morning with your mind churning. You know the routine.

Brain Brief

In their research examining the biological effects of mindfulness meditation, Jon Kabat-Zinn and Richard Davidson found that in addition to a shift to greater happiness, participants in an eight-week MBSR program also showed an enhanced immune response to an influenza vaccine.

Knowing When to Rest Your Case

There is a time for many words and there is also a time for sleep.

Homer

The Importance of Sleep

- Great trial attorneys know when to rest their case. Many ill-fated trials were lost when attorneys did not have this instinct and put on that one-too-many witness or asked that one-too-many question.

- There is wisdom in knowing when to say, "Your Honor, I rest my case."

- In law school, the temptation to keep on going can prove detrimental to your mind and body. Rather than seeing sleep as an impediment to good grades and high performance, you can use sleep to accelerate your learning and performance.

MINDFULNESS MEMO

Being mindfully aware of your mind and body allows you to develop the insight and wisdom to know when it is time to sleep or take a tactical nap. Practicing mindfulness will make it easier for you to fall asleep and benefit from the 3 R's, a Restful, Rejuvenating, and Rewiring slumber.

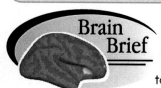

Brain Brief Research on the benefits of rest, be it taking a quick nap or a good night's sleep, are well documented. Done smartly, rest can facilitate your retention and recall of information.

- **A good night's sleep promotes insight.** A group of students were taught to solve a group of problems, which unbeknown to them could be solved though a shortcut. Twelve hours later, they were asked to solve some more. Those students given eight hours to rest after the initial training were three times more likely to experience a flash of insight and figure out the shortcut.

- **Study while you sleep.** When rats are taught to navigate a maze, their brain cells fire off in a specific pattern. When the rats sleep, this pattern is then replayed again and again, reinforcing the information.

Brain Brief: Supplemental Brief

- **Problem solving:** People given a mathematical puzzle before bed were twice as likely to find a shortcut to the solution after getting a good night's sleep. So, the next time someone wants to stay up extra late for a study review and wants to know "right now," tell them you need to "Sleep on it!"

- **Cognitive-enhancing naps.** A NASA study showed that a 26-minute nap improved a pilot's performance by 34 percent. Make it a 45-minute nap and the jump in performance lasts six hours.

- **Lack of sleep affects cognitive function.** The performance of soldiers responsible for complex military hardware was tested after they pulled an all-nighter. The next day they experienced a 30 percent loss in overall cognitive skill. Pull another all-nighter and suffer a 60 percent decline. And get this—if sleep was limited to six hours a night for one week, their cognitive skills were as poor as those subjected to 48 hours of sleep deprivation.

Exercising Your Rights

It is exercise alone that supports the spirits and keeps the mind in vigor.

Cicero

Brain Fitness

- The law is all about rights. The exercise of civil rights and human rights make for a just and enlightened society.

- It's the same with physical exercise, which has long been known to improve mood, clarity of mind, and health. It may also specially activate the right side of your brain.

- Science is offering further evidence that exercise is also a boon to your brain, promoting neuroplasticity and cognitive functioning.

MINDFULNESS MEMO

You can bring mindful awareness to your exercise routine—enhancing its effectiveness. A classic mindfulness exercise is yoga. Often "on all fours," yoga is considered by many to be mindfulness of the breath with movement wrapped around it. The same can be said for all exercise.

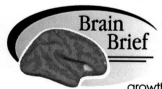

Brain Brief

Given the current student appetite for adderal, a sizeable market surely would exist for brain-derived neurotrophic factor (BDNF), a chemical that enriches the neurons in your hippocampus. Called Miracle-Gro for its extraordinary brain growth properties, BDNF make dendrites bushy—and ready and able to form new neural connections. While you can't buy BDNF at the health food store, you can generate it yourself with . . . exercise.

- **Faster learning.** Aerobic production increases BDNF production. A recent study showed that people learned vocabulary words 20 percent faster after exercise than they did before exercise. Moreover, the rate at which they learned correlated with levels of BDNF.

- **Study after exercise.** To enhance the benefits of exercising on your GPA, study intellectually stimulating material after exercise. For one thing, blood flow returns to your brain enhancing learning. For another, dendrites, bushy from exercise, get wired into neural circuitry. You have a smarter brain for the long term and better learn the material.

61

Brain
Brief: Supplemental Brief

- **Nourish your memory.** Neuroscientists at Columbia University had a group of men and women, ages 21-45, work out for one hour four times a week. After 12 weeks, almost twice as much blood was being sent to each person's hippocampus. The subjects all showed significant improvements in memory tests, with the amount of increased blood flow in direct proportion to their improvement.

- **Reduce anxiety.** Exercise increases levels of dopamine in the brain, which improves mood and enhances your ability to pay attention in class and while studying. Exercise also increases levels of serotonin which is important not just for mood, but also impulse control and feelings of self-worth. Serotonin also helps control the release of cortisol, calming the amygdala and reducing stress.

- **Help with ADHD.** John Ratey, an expert on ADHD and the role of exercise on the brain, writes that exercise can help regulate ADHD through the release of the neurotransmitters dopamine and norepinephrine.

Food Court Battles

Only a small percentage of what we eat nourishes us;
the balance goes to waste and loss of energy.

Sir William Osler

Difficult Decisions to Digest

- Finding time to eat in between classes, study sessions, and sleep can be challenging. Often it involves grabbing the "fastest" food and consuming it in the car, while watching television, surfing the Internet, or studying.

- Eating can be a distraction from unpleasant feelings like anxiety. It can also feed into a physiology primed for fats and sugars.

- Mindful eating involves cultivating awareness of the thoughts and feelings that precede an impulse toward "automatic" eating, which often leads to the consumption of too much food, and of foods you did not want to eat.

MINDFULNESS MEMO

When you eat mindfully, you bring awareness to your thoughts, feelings, and bodily sensations. You might ask yourself, "How hungry am I?" Answering this question, you learn something about yourself in that moment. You intentionally slow down the conditioned movements of your hands and mouth, and create the opportunity to taste, smell, see, and feel—to savor—the experience. You relate differently to eating, disrupting old patterns. You also may find you enjoy the experience more and eat more in line with your nutritional needs.

Brain Brief

Mindful eating can result in the consumption of less food, as there is greater awareness of feeling sated and of self-soothing tendencies.

- The Proceedings of the National Academy of Sciences reported that memory can improve on a calorie-restricted diet. Since so many overeat, mindful eating may naturally signal a calorie-appropriate diet, along with the memory benefits associated with caloric reduction.

- In a study conducted at Duke and Indiana State University, binge eaters who participated in a nine-week mindful-eating program went from binging an average of four times a week to just once, and reduced their levels of insulin resistance, a precursor to diabetes.

Preliminary Hearing

Music is a moral law. It gives soul to the universe, wings to the mind, flight to the imagination, and charm and gaiety to life and to everything.

Plato

Time for Sound Judgment

- Listening to music can be an enjoyable way to relax, focus, and practice mindfulness.

- There are many different types of music, and they have different influences on your nervous system.

- The art of mindful listening is that the listening is preliminary to thinking about the music. You are just listening, absorbing the sound without judgment.

MINDFULNESS MEMO

Listening to music makes a great mindfulness exercise. Play soothing sounds, perhaps classical, or some slow-tempo music to feel calming effects. Add to this relaxing component, awareness of the sound and vibration of the notes, the feelings that the music brings up within you, and other sensations that are happening "in the moment" as you listen. As you become aware of thoughts arising, gently bring your attention back to the music. Breathe.

Brain Brief

- Research has shown that rhythmic music has a profound effect on your mind and body. Music has been found to help with attention deficit disorders, anxiety, and depression; it also boosts immunity, and eases muscle tension.

- At a symposium at Stanford, researchers discussed how music with a strong beat can stimulate brain waves to resonate in sync with the beat, with faster beats bringing sharper concentration and more alert thinking, and a slower tempo promoting a calm, relaxing state.

- Music can result in slower breathing, slower heart rate, and an activation of the relaxation response, helping alleviate the damaging effects of chronic stress.

The "In a Sense" Project

> *To live is not merely to breathe: it is to act; it is to make use of our organs, senses, faculties —of all those parts of ourselves which give us the feeling of existence.*
>
> **Jean-Jacques Rousseau**

Early Release from Mental Chatter

- The *Innocence Project* is an organization dedicated to exonerating wrongly convicted people and preventing future injustices.

- When you become so caught up in your mind that you lose touch with your body, you run the risk of becoming trapped in rigid thinking patterns and excessive mental chatter.

- This can compromise sound decision making because the prefrontal cortex is in overdrive, inhibiting a more balanced neural give and take.

- Learning to be more aware of your senses can free you from these constraints.

MINDFULNESS MEMO

In his book, *Coming to Our Senses,* Jon Kabat-Zinn writes: "(W)e know from many studies in mind/body medicine in the past thirty years that it is possible to come to some degree of peace within the body and mind and so find greater health, well-being, happiness, and clarity, even in the midst of great challenges and difficulties. . . . Coming to our senses is the work of no time at all, only of being present and awake here and now."

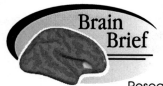

Brain Brief

A mindfulness exercise that can help you exercise your mindfulness muscle is the Body Scan (see page 102). It is one of three exercises included in the MBSR program and has a history that goes back thousands of years.

Research is beginning to look at the effect of this specific practice. A preliminary study conducted by Harvard neuroscientist Catherine Kerr has shown that brain wave activity measured by MEG scans—specifically alpha waves associated with attention—changed after practicing a body scan for three weeks.

Aromatherapy & the Nose that Knows

Take time to smell the roses.

Proverb

The Sweet Smell of Success

- In the law, the "smell test" is used to assess the legitimacy of a legal theory or course of conduct. You don't want to fail the smell test.

- One smell test that is easy to pass, and can be beneficial to your health and performance in law school, is aromatherapy.

- Aromatherapy involves the use of selected fragrances to affect mood and promote health, and has been shown to carry many wellness and stress-relief benefits.

MINDFULNESS MEMO

The sense of smell is one of your earliest-developed sense perceptions, and one of the most finely attuned. Because scents are associated with areas of the brain related to emotions, they often trigger emotionally rich memories. The olfactory sense can disrupt automatic thinking, and can be helpful in "bringing you to your senses."
Because it is common to relate to scents through description and comparison, the mindfulness challenge is to not confuse the bare experience of smelling with judging what you smell.

 **Brain Brief**

Preliminary research shows that aromatherapy can:

- Alter brain waves and behavior.

- Reduce the perception of stress, increase contentment, and decrease levels of the stress hormone cortisol.

- Have beneficial effects on anxiety and depression.

- Offer relief from mental fatigue.

Unlike American jurisprudence where all people are created equal, in aromatherapy, not all scents are created equal. On the following page, you'll find examples of how you might use different scents. It's a nice way to turn your home into a spa. Even your car can become a sanctuary.

Mindfulness Exercise: Aromatherapy

The primary ways of experiencing aromatherapy are through oils, candles, and diffusers. You can find them in health food stores, online, and even at your grocery and drugstore. Get a scented candle or a diffuser and oil and away you go. Be careful if you use matches; the benefits of the aromatherapy are likely to be outweighed by the cortisol surge if your apartment burns down.

Rosemary (Reducing Stress). Rosemary has been found to have positive effects on performance and mood, and it also may reduce cortisol levels.

Lavender (Cognitive Performance and Sleep). Lavender may help you feel content and improve your mood. It may also enhance your cognitive performance. It too can reduce cortisol levels. And, get this—it has been shown to promote deep sleep in men and women.

Peppermint (Enhancing Memory). Peppermint is associated with an increase in memory and alertness. Remember, if what you said in class is not what you "meant" to say, then get mint to say what you mean.

Ylang-ylang (Calming, But Buyer Beware). While ylang-ylang is a terrific scent and has been found to promote calmness and reduce stress, it has also been found to decrease alertness, impair memory, and slightly lengthen processing speed. Enjoy it when you want to chill out.

Lemon (Anti-Depressant). Lemon oil may possess anti-depressant-type factors. So, the next time you find you bought something that was a lemon, you need not get overly depressed about it . . . as long as it really *is* a lemon.

Daily Practice

As you know, not enough can be said about the importance of taking care of your mind and body. While this can be challenging when the heat of cramming or the stress of feeling worried or overwhelmed take hold, there are choices you have that you can implement, both in advance of these moments and during them. Of course, it is most diffi-cult in the midst of challenge. So start now. After all, *there is no time like the present.*

Case in Point:

Karen was all over the place. "Sometimes I was in control, other times I felt out of control. My eating and sleeping would be fine and then I would get stressed and I would regress to fast food and late nights. And forget exercise. That would have to wait. I really didn't have control. It would just happen. But then I read up on how all three affected my mood and I realized that it was my mood that was making me think I had to eat fast, and sleep only after I couldn't stay awake any longer. Hearsay! I was squeezed out of the decision. Knowing that eating better, sleep-ing and taking naps, and exercise would actually help me study and learn, I got back into the driver's seat. The aromatherapy helped me remember, and I had great aromas in my home and car to help me relax and keep me on track.

Daily Practice:

Review the sections in this chapter and select the one that res-onates or strikes you at a gut level. Make the intention to incor-porate it into your life this next week.

Exercise:

Practice the *Just Is Holmes* exercise on page 98. Do so while lis-tening to easy, relaxing music.

Resources

Books

Elwark, A., *Stress Management for Lawyers* (Vorkell, 2007).

Kabat-Zinn, J., *Coming to Our Senses* (Hyperion, 2005).

Medina, J., *Brain Rules* (Pear Press, 2008).

Ratley, J., *Spark: The Revolutionary New Science of Exercise and the Brain* (Little Brown, 2008).

Worwood, V., *The Complete Book of Essential Oils and Aromatherapy* (New World Library, 1991).

Articles

Beck, M., "Putting an End to Mindless Munching," *Wall Street Journal* (May 13, 2008).

Belluck, P., "Another Potential Benefit of Cutting Calories: Better Memory," *New York Times* (January 26, 2009).

Edmund O. & Panteleimon E., "Psychobiology of Physical Activity," in *Physical Activity, Affect & Electroencephalogram Studies,* 123, ed. Pettruzello, Ekkekakis & Hall.

Hobson, K., "Can Mindful Eating Help You Lose Weight," *U.S. News and World Report* (March 5, 2009).

Kabat-Zinn, J., Davidson, R., et al., "Alterations in Brain and Immune Function Produced by Mindfulness Meditation," *Psychosomatic Medicine* 65:564—570 (2003).

Kerr, C., Paper presented at the Seventh Annual International Scientific Conference for Clinicians, Researchers and Educators Investigating and Integrating Mindfulness in Medicine, Health Care and Society (March 19, 2009).

Kraut, R., "Music Listening to Facilitate Relaxation and Promote Wellness: Integrated Aspects of our Neurophysiological Responses to Music," *The Arts in Psychotherapy*, (34) 134—141 (2007).

CHAPTER 7

Ethics and Professionalism

The ethical and professional behavior of law students and lawyers is important both to society and to the well-being of the practitioner. While there is much attention on teaching and enforcing the rules of conduct, less is paid to helping one navigate through their inherent ambiguities. This is complicated further as mentors and colleagues cross gray lines, justified by what historically has been expressed as the obligation to provide "zealous" advocacy. The perception, real or imagined, that one's opponent is engaging in unprofessional or unethical conduct further complicates matters, as an unwillingness to engage in a *quid pro quo* may be perceived as weak or ineffectual.

Professor Lawrence Krieger makes the important point that great stress can follow conduct that is out of line with one's core values. Yet time and again attorneys have surprised themselves and their colleagues by losing touch with their core values and engaging in improper conduct. The list of well-regarded lawyers hitting bottom continues to grow.

This chapter looks to the influence of interpersonal dynamics on conduct. *Meeting of the Minds* explores the role of empathy and insight in establishing a bridge between you and your classmates, mentors, adversaries, and even judges and juries. *Quid Pro Quo* is a reminder of how you may be affected and subtly influenced by others' conduct, and to the discovery of "mirror neurons" that may mediate this process. *The Slippery Slope* cautions that steps you take into shaky professional terrain may create or reinforce neural pathways that encourage more of the same. Finally, *Res Ipsa Loquitur* offers one method of relief and transformation—the power of silence, both as a tool for effective advocacy and as a mechanism to create space between you and thoughts or actions you may come to regret.

Meeting of the Minds

The spirit of liberty is the spirit which seeks to understand the minds of other men and women. . . .

Judge Learned Hand

Knowing the Mind of Another

- A valid contract or agreement calls for a "meeting of the minds."

- Most disagreements are the product of two minds misunderstanding one another.

- Mindfulness practices can alter the structure and function of the brain so that there is more attuned communication and greater empathy—facilitating a true meeting of the minds.

MINDFULNESS MEMO

Two domains that have been linked to mindfulness meditation are empathy and insight. *Empathy* refers to intuiting the mind of another —a classmate, a professor, an interviewer. This trait is the basis for communication and compassion. Just about everyone can cultivate greater empathy through mindfulness practices. *Insight* is the complement of empathy—knowing your own mind. When empathy and insight arise together, you know the mind of another along with your own. This is a true "meeting of the minds." You may recognize this moment when you are feeling attuned and connected to another person—or at one with yourself. It is a skill you can develop that will benefit you throughout your career and in many aspects of life.

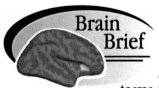

Brain Brief

In his book, *The Mindful Brain*, Dan Siegel notes that mindfulness meditation can stimulate the brain's middle prefrontal regions (see page 25), and play a role in the development of empathy and insight, which he terms "mindsight." The more you practice mindfulness, the more you cultivate these qualities, important in so many aspects of your life.

Quid Pro Quo

> *[I]f you see me choke up, in emotional distress from striking out at home plate, mirror neurons in your brain simulate my distress. You automatically have empathy for me. You know how I feel because you literally feel what I am feeling.*
>
> **Giacomo Rizzolatti, PhD**

Remembering Who You Are

- *Quid pro quo* means "something for something." You give and you get. It is often applied to interpersonal exchanges and interactions.

- Consider how often your interactions with others tend to be mutually regarded—joyful and connected, neutral, irritated and disconnected.

- *Quid pro quo* is a reminder of our connectedness—of the subtle ways we influence each other. Neuroscience is beginning to identify areas in the brain, called "mirror neurons," that engage during social interactions and may play a role in influencing professional conduct.

MINDFULNESS MEMO

The Zen Master, Thich Nhat Hanh, tells the story of the panic that ensued when villagers being attacked were escaping into rickety old boats. Overloaded and filled with screams and cries from parents and children, boats would capsize and sink, drowning everyone on board. But, Thich Nhat Hanh teaches, if one person on a boat were able to remain grounded and present, others would respond in kind, and it could save the entire boat.

Brain Brief

Mirror neurons are brain cells that respond to the intentions and actions of others. Serendipity revealed them. An electrode was hooked up to a single motor neuron in a monkey's brain, firing when the monkey reached for a peanut. One day the monkey saw another monkey reach for a peanut. Unexpectedly, this triggered the monkey's motor neuron to fire, transforming our understanding of how people may influence each other. One of the keys to mirror neuron activation appears to be action that is associated with an intention. Ethical and professional conduct is about as intentional as it gets. Your classmates' conduct may be activating mirror neurons in your brain. Being mindful of this phenomenon can help you remain stable in choppy waters.

The Slippery Slope

> *It is unwise to be too sure of one's own wisdom. It is healthy to be reminded that the strongest might weaken and the wisest might err.*
>
> ### *Gandhi*

Losing Your Honor

- The "slippery slope" is a caution that a legal decision may have unintended and undesirable consequences, and that if implemented a momentum builds, leading to more and more unintended outcomes.

- The neuroplastic features of the brain have a *slippery slope* quality as well. As your conduct changes, neural grooves and pathways are rewired to support and reinforce the conduct, and your intentions.

- An understanding of mirror neurons, i.e., your neural connection to other people, and susceptibility to their actions, can be helpful in avoiding the *slippery slope* into improper, unprofessional, and even unethical conduct.

MINDFULNESS MEMO

It is common for lawyers to complain about the conduct of opposing counsel. This "perception" can lead lawyers to feel that they've been dragged into the muck and that it is necessary to fight fire with fire in order to effectively represent their client. In subtle ways, these lawyers may find themselves engaged in a neural *Quid Pro Quo* where their "bad conduct" neurons are firing, leading them to engage in questionable legal tactics.

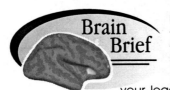

Brain Brief

Neurologist Alvaro Pascual-Leone cautions that the "mental tracks" that get laid down can lead to habits, good or bad." The brain changes in response to experience, plain and simple. So, be attentive to the character and requests of your legal mentors for, as research into mirror neurons suggest, you learn from them on both the inside and outside. Moreover, be mindful of the actions of your classmates, for their conduct too can shape your own. One antidote for these subtle influences that can have dramatic consequences is to remain mindful—attentive to your thoughts, feelings, and sensations. From time to time, inquire "mirror, mirror in my brain . . . ."

Res Ipsa Loquitur

> *All of man's problems are caused by his inability to sit quietly in a room by himself.*
>
> **Pascal**

The Professionalism of Silence

- *Res ipsa loquitur* means "the thing speaks for itself." This doctrine entered the law in response to a set of facts that were regarded as too obvious to warrant debate.

- *Res ipsa loquitur* also means to allow the truth to speak for itself—saying what needs to be said and no more.

MINDFULNESS MEMO

Silence is a powerful mindfulness tool. It surfaces naturally when nothing more needs to be said. It is deliberately introduced into mindfulness meditations as a mechanism for insight. Whether contemplating your own mind, or in relationship with another, your willingness to deliberately introduce silence—when you could be asserting yourself—has powerful transformative qualities. You intentionally disrupt your own mind's reactivity. In doing so, you disrupt the reactivity of those around you. You will be surprised at how silence can bring about greater presence and insight (or at least a surprising acquiescence), even among your adversaries.

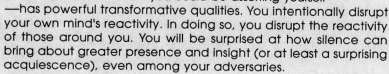

Brain Brief

When you catch your mind in agitation and reactivity and choose to respond with silence (not to be confused with being frozen into silence), you begin to change the pathways of your brain to reinforce a less reactive pattern. This becomes easier in time. It also strengthens your concentration and attention skills. You become more focused and less distractible.

Mindfulness Exercise:
Silence in the Neural Circuit Courtroom

There are two forms of silence you can practice in daily discourse that can have a profound impact on the quality of your interactions, your effectiveness at work and home, and the cultivation of greater concentration and focus. Not surprisingly, you may also see positive changes in your steadiness and sense of well-being.

The first is to not react verbally—to say nothing—when you find yourself agitated. Generally, if you are feeling agitated, the person you are interacting with is feeling uncomfortable too. Rather than facilitate further reactivity, introduce silence. Not only might this save you from saying something you'll regret, but it also lifts a huge burden as you instead take a deep breath and sink into the moment. This is a type of "silence as acceptance," meaning an acceptance of the moment as it "Just Is." See if you can be receptive and open to what happens next.

In time, you will become less reactive and begin to see reactivity brewing in others. At these moments of clarity, you can introduce silence to ease another's reactive spirit, or speak from a place of greater presence—both of which elevate the interaction.

The second form is to insert a deliberate pause, a *But-for-Pause*, before you speak. In the space of a few seconds, you have the opportunity to dissipate intense emotional charge and to reflect on responses otherwise concealed by the weight of reactive impulses. Notice what emerges in the space you create, both in terms of your own mind and the conduct of others.

These practices are equally applicable when interacting with another over the phone, or via e-mail and text messaging.

Daily Practice

Mindfulness plays a significant role in the evolution of your ethical and professional fiber (and the associated neural fibers). Remaining aware of your core values—and professional responsibilities—and mindfully attending to whether your thoughts, feelings, and actions are in line with them can be career saving and stress relieving. Bringing awareness to how your connection with others can influence your state of mind is a pivotal insight.

Case in Point:

One of America's great trial lawyers, Robert Josefsberg, shares with students and attorneys the metaphor of a mythical clay cube with eight corners, to illustrate the effect of unprofessional and unethical conduct. The cube resides in the brain with a pole running through its axis. Each time you make a deliberate misrepresentation or engage in conduct that is contrary to your values, the cube rotates. At first, the friction between the cube's corners and surrounding gray matter is felt (that gnawing feeling of knowing you're doing something wrong), generating awareness and an opportunity for self-corrective action. But if ignored, the corners, made of mortar, slowly erode to the point that the cube becomes a sphere, spinning freely. As it turns out, this ancient metaphor is a beautiful expression of neuroplasticity.

Daily Practice:

- When interacting with your peers, take a moment and observe them. Remove yourself from the exchange. Study their faces and gestures and see if you can detect what they are feeling. Pay attention to your thoughts, feelings, and bodily sensations.

Exercise:

- Practice 4—7—8 Hands Plus (see page 94). This exercise can be especially helpful when you find yourself becoming worried. It is during times of fear that people are susceptible to choosing improper conduct with short-term benefits and long-term adverse consequences.

- Read the Motion to Recuse found on page 112.

Resources

Books

Begley, S., *Train Your Mind, Change Your Brain: How a New Science Reveals Our Extraordinary Potential to Transform Ourselves* (Ballantine Books, 2007).

Cozolino, L., *The Neuroscience of Human Relationships* (Norton, 2006).

Daicoff, S., *Lawyer, Know Thyself* (APA, 2004).

Iacoboni, M., *Mirroring People: The New Science of How We Connect with Others* (Farrar, Strauss and Giroux, 2008).

Kauffman, G., *The Lawyer's Guide to Balancing Life & Work: Taking the Stress Out of Success* (ABA, 2006).

Keeva, S., *Transforming Practices: Finding Joy and Satisfaction in the Legal Life* (Contemporary Books, 1999).

Krieger, L., *The Hidden Sources of Law School Stress* (2005, booklet for law students).

Siegel, D., *The Mindful Brain: Reflection and Attunement in the Cultivation of Well-Being.* (Norton, 2006).

Articles

Blakeslee, S., "Cells That Read Minds," *New York Times* (January 10, 2006).

Websites

UM Law Center for Ethics and Public Service,
www.law.miami.edu/ceps/

CHAPTER 8

Sitting In (and Out of) Judgment

Traditional contemplative practices, such as mindfulness, involve sitting meditation. The benefits of sitting for 5, 10, or 20 minutes once or twice a day can be profound. Pascal's insight that "all of man's problems are caused by his inability to sit quietly in a room by himself," is not a mandate that people sit quietly in a room by themselves, but a comment on the fact that most people can't—at least, not without experiencing inner turmoil, commonly labeled "boredom."

Throughout this book you have been reminded of the mind's wandering and reactive spirit. Perhaps this led to insight into the nature of your own mind and how you can get in the way of achieving your objectives.

Many of the *Learned Hand Exercises* and *Daily Practices* offer you ways of slowing down and catching your reactive mind in action, and of moving into greater mindful awareness during such moments. These are insights and exercises that you can employ when the rubber meets the road during challenging school-related experiences.

A different kind of rubber meets the road when you take the time to sit in mindful contemplation. At first it looks like you are removing yourself from life's hustle and bustle. In fact, you are creating an environment in which to recognize and see more clearly the source of this hustle and bustle—your own mind.

Sitting in mindful meditation offers you a powerful method of relaxation and clarity—a great way to reset your chattering mind. But even more, it can enliven your awareness so that you pierce more deeply into the core of who you are—as a law student, a future lawyer, and a human being.

Watching the Wheels

I'm just sitting here watching the wheels go round and round.

John Lennon

Mindfulness Meditation

- Sitting in mindfulness meditation is a powerful method of cultivating greater mindful awareness, along with concentration and clarity.
- In John Lennon's song, "Watching the Wheels," he describes this practice.

I'm just sitting here watching the wheels go round and round.
I really love to watch them roll.
No longer riding on the merry-go-round. I just had to let it go.

MINDFULNESS MEMO

Law professor Leonard Riskin describes mindfulness meditation as:

"a way of paying attention moment to moment without judgment to whatever is going on in the mind and in the body—including thoughts, physical sensations, and emotions."

Paying attention to "whatever is going on in the mind" can mean "watching the wheels."

And when Lennon tells us he "really love(s) to watch them roll," he is letting us know that he's watching without judgment.

Freedom from the chatter of the mind comes when you can watch what arises and not get caught by it—when you can have thoughts and feelings that used to push your buttons and choose to "let it go."

When this happens, you "get off the merry-go-round" and watch the play of life, and love the play of life, but not get stifled or limited by it.

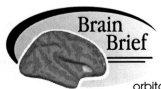

Brain Brief

Eileen Luders at UCLA's Laboratory of Neuro Imaging used high-resolution MRI to study the brains of long-term meditators and found significantly larger volumes of the right hippocampus and increased gray matter in the right orbitofrontal cortex, the right thalamus, and the left inferior temporal lobe. Luders noted that because these areas are linked to emotions, "these might be the neuronal underpinnings that give meditators the outstanding ability to regulate their emotions and allow for well-adjusted responses to whatever life throws their way."

Mindfulness Exercise: Sitting Meditation

As a formal sitting practice, find a time to sit for 5, 10, or 15 minutes. Ideally, this time will be available on a regular basis, should you find this practice beneficial.

The instruction below will guide you through the meditation—as you sit and watch the wheels go round and round. It's a powerful experience which, as you've learned in this book, changes your brain—can make you a more effective student—can boost your immune system—can increase your well-being. While you may begin "on the cushion," or your kitchen chair, you carry your mind with you wherever you go, and so the insights and benefits of the practice are with you throughout your life.

Instructions:

1. Find a comfortable place to sit. If in a chair, place your feet flat on the ground.
2. Close your eyes (or lower them, if you prefer).
3. Allow your hands to rest together or on your lap.
4. Bring awareness to your breathing, and observe it.
5. Bring awareness to your in-breath, to the feel of the air as it enters your nose or mouth, or to the rise of your belly. Allow your belly to ride easy with the breath.
6. In the same way, bring awareness to your out-breath.
7. If you find that your mind wandered, that's fine. That's what the mind does. Simply and gently bring your mind back to your breath.
8. Treat your thoughts as if they were clouds passing across the sky. No one stops the clouds. No need to try to stop the thoughts. Allow them to be just as they are.
9. You can observe that you are having a thought by silently noting to yourself "ah, thought," and then returning to your breathing.

The Neural Circuit Courthouse

> *Mindfulness is cultivated by assuming the stance of impartial witness to your own experience.*
>
> **Jon Kabat-Zinn**

Observing Life's Trials & Tribulations

- The participants in a trial can include a judge, jury, prosecutor, defendant, victim, eyewitness, expert, police, interpreter, and so on.

- Many of these "personalities" can be found arising in your mind. They chime in to explain events and people.

- If you do not realize they are chiming in, you may automatically start believing them—and living your life according to their biased perception.

- With awareness you can observe these "well-intended" mind states as they arise and not get caught up in their drama. Then, you are free to make decisions, less influenced by conditioning, preconception, and agenda.

MINDFULNESS MEMO

You can view your mind as a courthouse. How many times has a situation arisen where you found yourself the "expert" or the "victim" or gone on the "defense"? How many times have you "judged" or "interpreted" events? Jon Kabat-Zinn suggests one method of relating differently to these critical voices is by taking on the attitude of an *impartial witness.* Doing so, you have an easier time recognizing inner dialogues as a series of mental events—often arising out of your conditioned past, and not necessarily as objective reality. Objection: "Hearsay."

One of the best ways to develop this clarity into your true nature is to sit. Just as you watch the wheels in sitting meditation, you can imagine yourself as that impartial witness, looking around at all the characters in the courtroom, marveling over how each does their job just right.

The courtroom is, of course, your life, with its many and never-ending trials and tribulations. Sit in your chair and watch the drama, enjoy the hype and fanfare, and maintain your deeper awareness and insight that this is your mind's reactivity. Watching the wheels tends to slow them down. The slower the wheels, the more detail you can see—the more insight that can flow, and the more freedom you can achieve.

Four Prayers for Relief

Peace is not the absence of war; it is a virtue; a state of mind; a disposition for benevolence, confidence, and justice.

Spinoza

Charitable Contributions

- All complaints filed in court contain a prayer for relief.

- Prayers for relief occasionally can be couched in terms that are equitable and mutually beneficial.

- The *Four Prayers For Relief* wish (1) happiness, (2) health, (3) safety, and (4) ease of heart for oneself and others.

- Neuroscience research is finding that when you deliberately wish well for other people, your brain activity changes and you can become happier.

MINDFULNESS MEMO

A mindfulness practice known as "cultivating loving kindness" invites you to wish yourself and others well. The Four Prayers for Relief (see page 84) is a loving-kindness meditation that you can practice during times of quiet and ease as well as when things get rough. It serves as a heart-opening quality that can tone down feelings of anger, resentment, and fear. It can also help tone down self-criticism and doubt. You will find yourself better equipped to deal with difficult people.

Brain Brief

Neuroscientist Richard Davidson asked monks who had meditated for thousands of hours to practice loving-kindness meditation while hooked up to EEG machines. He also asked non-meditators to do the same. He found that everyone experienced a shift of neural activity to the left anterior portion of the brain. This shift has been found to be associated with happiness. Not surprisingly, the changes in brain activity were significantly more pronounced in the monks. Interestingly, these changes persisted after the meditation stopped, suggesting that this practice can lead to lasting changes in the brain.

Mindfulness Exercise:
The Four Prayers for Relief

The *Four Prayers for Relief* ask for one to be:

1. Happy
2. Healthy
3. Safe, and to
4. Live with Ease of Heart.

It is directed to:

1. Oneself
2. A Benefactor
3. A Neutral Person
4. A Difficult Person
5. All Beings

Instructions:

1. Find a comfortable posture. Close or lower your eyes and bring awareness to your breathing. Follow your breath for a few cycles. If your mind wanders, simply note that it is restless and return to the breath. You can also apply this practice in whole or part anytime during the day—perhaps when with friends or during a challenging time.

2. Bring to mind an image or sense of yourself in the present moment and wish for yourself the *Four Prayers for Relief*. Breathe.

3. Bring to mind a close friend or benefactor and wish for them the *Four Prayers for Relief*. Breathe.

4. Repeat this for a neutral person—someone you briefly encountered but do not really know at all. Breathe.

5. Bring to mind a difficult person—for example, someone you are angry at or have a difficult time interacting with, and wish for them the *Four Prayers for Relief*. Breathe.

6. Bring to mind all living beings and wish relief for them. Breathe.

Koan, You Can Do It

The intellect has little to do on the road to discovery. There comes a leap in consciousness, call it intuition if you will, and the answer comes to you and you don't know how or why.

Albert Einstein

What is the Sound of One "Learned Hand" Clapping?

- As a law student, you cherish your ability to think through a problem, to break it down to its fundamental parts, develop a method of solving it, and arrive at a solution. This skill serves you well.

- Sometimes, however, a solution is not to be found by applying a familiar method. You can rack your brains and get nowhere. You become frustrated and old friends like doubt and hesitation come knocking. When they do, you can lose your edge and your effectiveness can be compromised.

- A Zen Koan is designed to help you get out of your mind and find solutions in places you might not have previously thought to look, or even known existed.

MINDFULNESS MEMO

A *Koan* (rhymes with "go on"), is an ancient Zen practice designed to help cultivate a different way of knowing. Working with koans (perhaps the most famous koan is "What is the sound of one hand clapping?"), you come to appreciate the futility of using problem-solving techniques that rely too much on "thinking." The mind eventually lets go and additional ways of knowing emerge—intuition, wisdom, insight.

Your Moment of Zen

In jurisprudence or a related course you likely learned that before there were laws, humans lived in a State of Nature. Yikes! Then, everyone entered into a social compact in which they gave up some of their liberty and empowered a sovereign to govern and regulate society. Here is a koan to ponder.

"Where is the State in a State of Nature?"

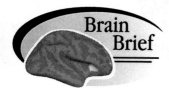

James Austin, MD, professor of neurology, decades-long student of Zen, and author of *Zen and the Brain*, reports that koans helped him "become more attentive, aware, and questioning."

Daily Practice

Mindfulness is a skill that offers benefits that permeate the whole of your life. In addition to providing clarity of mind, physical and emotional well-being, and the wisdom to navigate through challenging professional terrain, it cultivates a deepened sense of compassion, both for yourself and others.

The opportunities to become more mindfully aware are ever-present. You find them when you are taken by a bird's sudden call, or watch a leaf floating to the ground. As you have learned, you can choose to experience challenging moments from a place of awareness, observation, and allowing, and transform your relationship to them. You also find them in the observations of other people, just observing them in action, without judgment, seeing more clearly the majesty of life and its unfolding.

Case in Point:

- Don was open to sitting because he knew that there was a science behind it. Also he was Type A and very intense, so he could benefit from relaxation. When he first tried to meditate, he couldn't. *It was impossible for me to sit still for more than 15 seconds. My mind was racing and I literally kept feeling myself getting tugged to move, to stand up. And I did. At first that was the end of it and the meditation was over. Then, in time, I would stand and then take a breath and sit back down. When I did that I began to wonder who was tugging me. Me? But I wanted to sit. What was going on? Then I started to pay better attention to the instruction. To breathe. To watch myself breathe. To feel my body. To just stay put while my mind raced. And then, a few days into it, I felt this weight drop. It was a little easier for me to sit. And I realized it was my thoughts that were propelling me. "Get up." "You have to study NOW!" So I started to watch them. Great fun actually. And at that moment I knew something inside me changed. And I realized that that was a thought too.*

Daily Practice:

- Sit quietly in a room by yourself.

Resources

Books

Austin, J., *Zen and the Brain: Toward an Understanding of Meditation and Consciousness* (MIT Press, 1998).

Halpern, C., *Making Waves and Riding the Currents: Activism and the Practice of Wisdom* (Berrett-Koehler, 2008).

Kauffman, G., *The Lawyer's Guide to Balancing Life & Work: Taking the Stress Out of Success* (ABA, 2006).

Keeva, S., *Transforming Practices: Finding Joy and Satisfaction in the Legal Life* (Contemporary Books, 1999).

Articles

Cullen, L., "How to Get Smarter, One Breath at a Time," *Time* (January 10, 2006).

Green, P., "This is Your Brain on Happiness," *The Oprah Magazine* (March 2008).

Hyman, J. P., "The Mindful Lawyer: Mindfulness Meditation and Law Practice," *Vermont Bar Journal* (2007).

Luders, E., Toga, A., et al., "The Underlying Anatomical Correlates of Long-Term Meditation: Larger Hippocampal and Frontal Volumes of Gray Matter," *NeuroImage* 45:672—678 (2009).

Lutz, A., et al., "Long-Term Meditators Self-Induce High-Amplitude Gamma Synchrony During Mental Practice." PNAS, (2004).

Riskin, L., "The Contemplative Lawyer: On the Potential Contributions of Mindfulness Meditation to Law Students, Lawyers, and their Clients," 7 *Harvard Negotiation Law Review* 1—66 (2002).

Zeglovitch, R., "The Mindful Lawyer," *GPSolo Magazine*, (October/November 2006).

Websites

Center for Contemplative Mind in Society, www.contemplativemind.org/

CHAPTER 9

The Learned Hand Exercises

In this chapter you will find all of the *Learned Hand* exercises that are referenced in this book. While their discussion and application is intermingled throughout, they have been collected here for easy reference, so you may more readily grasp how they build upon each other.

They begin with the foundation mindfulness exercise of *Awareness of the Breath* and build with the addition of:

- counting *(4..7..8..10 Breathing)*
- the hands as an object of awareness *(Awareness of the Hands)*
- the combining of breath and hands *(4—7—8 Hands)*
- optimism *(4—7—8 Hands Plus)*
- mind-body connectedness *(Irresistible M-Pulse)*
- impermanence and connection *(The Three Judgments)*, and
- the whole body *(10-Minute Body Scan)*.

The primary exercise for daily use is *4—7—8 Hands.* Once this exercise becomes second nature, you will have an exercise you can use anytime to help you respond more effectively to challenging situations, and one that will help you reshape your brain's neural pathways.

You will also learn the *Just Is Holmes* and *Just Is Story* exercises, which are part of an advanced set of exercises called the *Hand Dial.* A shortened form of the *Hand Dial* is provided in this chapter. You can read a fuller treatment on *The Mindful Law Student* website.

The hands are the object of awareness for most of these exercises so that you can learn and apply them with greater ease. The hands are represented in the brain over a large expanse of neural real estate, which probably is not surprising given their extensive and consequential use in daily life. As a result, exercises involving awareness of the hands activate a good deal of the brain which may serve an important role in neuroplasticity.

All of these exercises are demonstrated on The Mindful Law Student website.

Awareness of the Breath

This breathing exercise is a foundation for all other *Learned Hand* exercises. As an object of contemplation, the breath goes back thousands of years and is found in practically every religious, spiritual, and contemplative domain.

Unlike the breathing you've done for most of your entire life, this exercise calls for *awareness* of breathing. It activates not just the back of your brain, but the front. Not just the reptile but the genius.

Breath awareness, also known as conscious breathing, involves learning to follow the movements of your in-breath and out-breath without trying to manipulate it or make it different than it is. This exercise will help you cultivate inner stillness and the ability to be present for your life, without judgment. As you practice it, allow yourself to feel the experience, from the inside out.

Instructions:

1. Sit in a chair, feet on the floor, hands resting on your lap.
2. Find a comfortable posture, not too rigid and not too relaxed.
3. Close your eyes and bring awareness to your breathing.
4. Place one of your hands atop your belly and feel it rise on the inhale and fall on the exhale.
5. Follow your breath as it repeats this rhythmic cycle.
6. Hold awareness on your breathing to the count of *ten*.
7. If you find that your mind has wandered, gently bring your attention back to your breathing. Continue counting where you left off or begin again.

COMMON QUESTIONS

I keep getting distracted on my way to ten. I can't seem to get to it.

Welcome to the club. That is a terrific insight. It is not important to get to ten. What is important is catching the wandering mind and bringing it back to the breath. That's one of the magic moments—maybe the most magical moment of mindfulness meditation.

4..7..8..10 Breathing

This variation on the foundation breathing exercise offers you an opportunity to fix your attention on an additional object---the count. You may find that it is easier, in that there is more going on to keep you engaged. You may find it more challenging.

The count itself, using 4—7—8, will help you remember those important three numbers which are used in the primary *Learned Hand* exercise.

Instructions:

1. Sit in a chair, feet on the floor, hands resting on your lap.
2. Find a comfortable posture, not too rigid and not too relaxed.
3. Close your eyes and bring awareness to your breathing.
4. Place one of your hands atop your belly and feel it rise on the inhale and fall on the exhale.
5. Follow your breath as it repeats this rhythmic cycle.
6. Hold awareness on your breathing to the count of *four*.
7. When you reach the count of four, exhale fully, releasing as much air as you can. Then continue on with the count.
8. When you reach the count of seven, exhale fully, releasing as much air as you can. Then continue on with the count.
9. When you reach the count of eight, exhale fully, releasing as much air as you can. Then continue on with the count until you reach ten.
10. If you find that your mind has wandered, gently bring your attention back to your breathing. Continue the count where you left off or begin again.

COMMON QUESTIONS

I feel like I am rushing to get to the next number. My breathing is strained.

That is a good observation and offers you the opportunity to stop trying to get it right. Don't try to control your breathing. You are just observing (until you reach the count and exhale fully). If you still find this difficult, simply stop making any effort to breathe until your body naturally draws in a breath. Then follow it from there.

Awareness of the Hands

This exercise incorporates the hands. You begin by bringing awareness to breathing and after a few breaths move your awareness to your hands, allowing it to rest there.

By incorporating the body, this exercise further develops your attention muscle. It also redistributes the energy that feeds a busy mind, and it readies you for the other *Learned Hand* exercises.

Instructions:

1. Sit in a chair, feet on the floor, hands resting on your lap.
2. Find a comfortable posture, not too rigid and not too relaxed.
3. Close your eyes and bring awareness to your breathing.
4. After a few cycles, move your awareness to your hands.
5. Sense their presence, visualize them, or feel them from the inside.
6. Continue to breathe as you sustain awareness in your hands.
7. When you realize that your mind has wandered, gently bring your attention back to your hands.
8. Hold awareness on your hands for a few minutes.

COMMON QUESTIONS

I have trouble sensing my hands.

That's okay. It can take a little while to establish this connection. See if wriggling your fingers or touching your fingertips together for a few seconds makes a difference.

4–7–8 Hands

This exercise, which you learned as part of the *Three-Tier Test* is reproduced here so that this chapter is complete. It builds on the *Awareness of the Hands* exercise by introducing movement. The movement follows a 4—7—8 count. The breathing portion goes back hundreds of years and is very helpful for anxiety and panic. Many people find the combination to be grounding and helpful in finding balance.

Practice this exercise both during times of calm and when in the midst of challenge. Find a time in the morning and evening to practice it—it takes about 30 seconds to repeat twice—as this will help you call on it with greater ease during moments of challenge.

Separate instructions are given for the hands and the breath so you can practice each first before putting them together. You may find the online demonstration helpful as it allows you to follow along.

Preliminary Instructions:

4–7–8 and the Breath
Inhale to the count of *four*. Hold your breath to the count of *seven*. Exhale to the count of *eight*.

4–7–8 and the Hands
Begin with your hands in a loose grip and fully extend your fingers to the count of *four*. Hold your fingers stretched open to the count of *seven*. Close your fingers, returning to a loose grip to the count of *eight*.

Instructions:

1. Sit in a chair—hands resting on your lap, palms face up in a gentle grip.
2. Bring awareness to your hands and to your breathing.
3. Inhale and extend your fingers fully to the count of *four*.
4. Hold your breath and keep your fingers extended to the count of *seven*.
5. Exhale and close your hands to the count of *eight*.
6. Repeat this exercise two to four times.

Tip: If comfortable, inhale through your nose and exhale through your mouth, as if blowing through a straw. On the exhalation, place your tongue on the roof of your mouth just behind your front teeth.

You can use also this exercise as a prelude to sitting meditation or practicing awareness of the breath.

4–7–8 Hands Plus

This exercise builds on the *4—7—8 Hands* exercise by introducing a deep sense of calm and optimism to the moment.

Before doing the exercise for the first time, find a relaxing position and close your eyes. Bring to mind someone who treated you with unconditional positive regard and love. They may be alive or might have passed away. If it is difficult to find this person, then think of someone you know or have heard about who you would have liked to be this person in your life.

Bring awareness to breathing for a few cycles as you sink into the moment. In your mind's ear, hear that person say to you: "Everything will be okay."

This exercise can be helpful when you find yourself forced to accept something that is unwanted or undesirable and you are feeling anxious, frustrated, or glum.

Instructions:

1. Do the *4—7—8 Hands* exercise twice with your eyes closed.
2. At the conclusion of the second cycle, after your palms return to a slight grip, extend your thumbs outward and pause.
3. Bring to mind the person and listen as their voice reassures you that "Everything will be okay."

COMMON QUESTIONS

What if I can't think of anyone like that?

You can also bring to mind a favorite pet. When you are asked to listen to them say "Everything will be okay," you can sense them sending you that message. People with close connections to pets are usually able to do this, so give it a try.

Irresistible M-Pulse

This exercise is a variation on *4—7—8 Hands* that furthers your connection to your body.

You begin by bringing awareness to your breathing. Then, use a thumb to detect your pulse at the wrist of your other hand (M-Pulse means My Pulse). Using the count of your own heartbeat, you breathe to 4—7—8.

Instructions:

1. Sit in a chair, feet on the floor, hands resting palms face up.
2. Find a comfortable posture, not too rigid and not too relaxed.
3. Bring awareness to your breathing.
4. Place the thumb of one hand on the wrist of your other hand and feel for your pulse.
5. When you've found the pulse, inhale fully to the count of *four* heartbeats.
6. Hold your breath to the count of *seven* heartbeats.
7. Exhale fully to the count of *eight* heartbeats.
8. Repeat this once.

COMMON QUESTIONS

I have trouble sensing my pulse.

That's okay. The pulse is fluid and will even change during the exercise. Sometimes it can be challenging to detect. If the time is not good, then practice the basic *4—7—8 Hands* exercise. But generally in a few moments—especially if you begin by bringing awareness to your breathing—you will find your pulse.

The more challenging event is when you lose your pulse during the exercise. If this happens, carry on using the tempo you had been following. You may detect your pulse again, but it is not necessary. The attention you bring to the exercise is the most important part.

The Hand Dial

This exercise is called the *Hand Dial* because just as a sundial brings awareness to the time of day, the *Hand Dial* bring awareness to your experience. It offers you an opportunity to transform any moment from one where life is happening to you to one where you are happening to life. The difference is paying attention, and the *Hand Dial* gently shifts your awareness from one state of mind to the other. You can draw on this exercise both during times of apparent calm and during challenging moments. It helps you catch your wandering mind and bring awareness back to the present moment.

The exercise is briefly discussed below. A more complete treatment can be found on The Mindful Law Student website. It is introduced to you here with special attention paid to two hand positions, the "*Just Is*" *Holmes* and the "*Just Is*" *Story* to give you a sense of how it is applied in practice. (See Illustration 9.1).

Instructions:

Select one hand and touch the tip of the thumb to the tip of the designated finger. You may want to take just a moment and attend to one finger, or use this as a longer meditation in which you move from finger to finger.

Touch Thumb to Pinkie, feeling the sensation of fingers touching and taking a breath. Bring awareness to the *sensations within the body*—merely opening to what is taking place within the body and allowing it.

Placing Thumb to Ring Finger, feeling the sensation of fingers touching and taking a breath. Then, awareness expands to embrace (or sense) a feeling of *connectedness*, that felt sense of being known, understood, and loved. It can be as simple as noting your connection to another person.

Placing Thumb to Middle Finger, feeling the sensation of fingers touching and taking a breath. Bring awareness to one of the *five senses* (sight, sound, smell, taste, touch) with a curious and alert mind. After a few breaths, you may want to explore another sense.

Placing Thumb to Forefinger, feeling the sensation of fingers touching and taking a breath. Then, look inward and note any *thoughts*, feelings, attitudes, or images that are arising in the mind, and witness them with a curious and open mind, allowing them to arise and pass away.

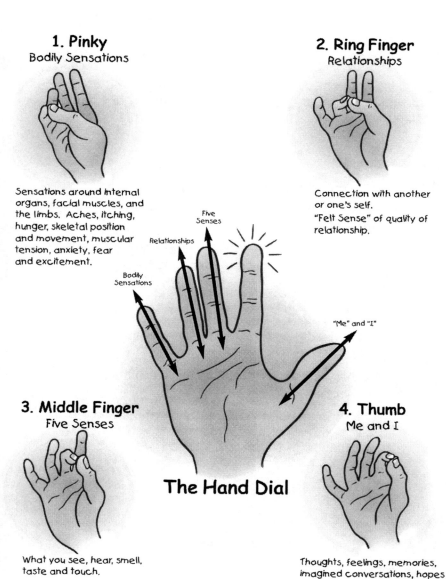

1. Pinky
Bodily Sensations

Sensations around internal organs, facial muscles, and the limbs. Aches, itching, hunger, skeletal position and movement, muscular tension, anxiety, fear and excitement.

2. Ring Finger
Relationships

Connection with another or one's self.
"Felt Sense" of quality of relationship.

Five Senses

Relationships

Bodily Sensations

"Me" and "I"

3. Middle Finger
Five Senses

The Hand Dial

What you see, hear, smell, taste and touch.

4. Thumb
Me and I

Thoughts, feelings, memories, imagined conversations, hopes and fears. I am angry, I am depressed, I am happy. Why is this happening to Me? I am Right. How dare you talk to Me like that.

Illustration 9.1

97

"Just Is" Holmes Exercise

You may recall the famous "stop, look, and listen" rule for a railroad crossing, laid down by Justice Holmes in 1927. The *"Just Is"* Holmes exercise invites you to "Stop," "Look," and "Listen" when you catch yourself becoming frustrated or feeling irritated or angry, or any other uncomfortable feelings.

Instructions:

1. Stop and bring awareness to breathing.

2. Touch together thumb and middle finger (i.e., the *Hand Dial* position for the five senses).

3. Soften your gaze. Allow awareness of breathing to move into the background as you bring awareness to the sights around you.

4. Really "see" what is there—colors, shapes, lights, shade, motion. . See if you can suspend judgment—by not identifying or assessing what you see—and simply be present for the arising, changing, and passing away of visual imagery.

5. Breathe. Allow awareness of sight to move into the background as you bring awareness to sound.

6. Really "listen" to sound—the murmur of an air-conditioning unit, people shuffling, voices, cars in motion and honking, the wind, your own breathing. Notice how it changes. Ceases. Reappears. Suspend judgment—by not identifying or assessing what you hear—and simply be present for the arising and passing away of sound.

Breathe.

Notice what *Just Is* taking place in the moment.

"Just Is" Story Exercise

Named after Justice Joseph Story, the *"Just Is" Story* exercise invites you to pay attention to the thoughts arising in your mind—the story you are telling yourself in the present moment.

This is a shortened version of a traditional mindfulness sitting meditation. It is one you can practice just about anywhere for any length of time.

It can be helpful to do so when you find yourself agitated, as this is often a time of prolific inner storytelling.

Instructions:

1. Bring awareness to breathing.

2. Touch together thumb and forefinger (i.e., the *Hand Dial* position for the stories you tell yourself).

3. Soften your gaze. Maintain awareness on breathing—observing the in-breath and the out-breath—for a few cycles.

4. Now turn inward toward the mind. Begin paying attention to the thoughts arising in the moment. Be patient.

5. Pay attention as an interested observer to the story you are telling yourself.

6. No need to do anything about it. The story "Just Is." No need to change anything. You need not agree or disagree, comment, revise, or judge.

7. Breathe and allow the moment to be as it "Just Is."

8. These are the thoughts crossing your mind. How interesting!

The Three Judgments

Constantly think of the Universe as one living creature, embracing one being and one soul; how all is absorbed into the one consciousness of this living creature; how it encompasses all things with a single purpose, and how all things work together to cause all that comes to pass, and their wonderful web and texture.

Marcus Aurelius

Joinder of all Parties

- Law school may at times, feel, in the words of Hobbes, "nasty, brutish and short"—well, maybe not short.

- During such times, it is common to feel separate and apart from a cohesive group. Events can quickly create the impression you are enemies with one another. Feelings of sadness, worry, or despair may arise.

- It can be helpful to remember a deep truth that we are all connected, we are all in this together, whether in law school, or life.

MINDFULNESS MEMO

It is easy to lose touch with our inner-connectedness. This is especially so in challenging environments where we keep up our guard, and remain vigilant to the next possible threat. Perceptions of who is friend and who is foe shift around. But the true nature of this world is one of connection. It can be helpful to remain mindful of this. *The Three Judgments* exercise on the following page is a reminder that all of life is constantly in flux and impermanent, as it is the true nature of all life to get sick, to grow old, and to die.

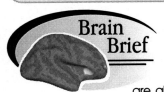

Brain Brief

Einstein understood the interconnected quality of all beings, commenting that the human tendency to forget this connection was an optical delusion of the mind. He wrote that the human condition was limited by "space and time," and that while we are all part of a greater "whole," perceptions of separateness — "a kind of optical delusion" of consciousness — can imprison the mind.

Just as *The Three Judgments* invites you to deepen your regard for others, Einstein recognized the importance of "widening our circle of compassion to embrace all living creatures." In conjunction with the *Four Prayers for Relief* (see page 83), this exercise embraces scientific research, which highlights the role compassion plays in one's own happiness and health.

The Three Judgments Exercise

You can do this powerful exercise at any time as a reminder of the impermanent and always-changing nature of life.

You can set aside time to practice it regularly—when waking up, before going to bed, at the gym or in traffic. You can also call upon it when angry or frustrated with someone—perhaps a professor or even yourself. Modify the personal pronoun to suit the context.

Instructions:

1. Bring awareness to breathing.

2. Make a fist with one of your hands, as if it were a judge's gavel. Slowly bring it to the open palm of your other hand and pronounce aloud or to yourself:

I will grow old.	**You will grow old.**	**We will grow old.**
I will get sick.	**You will get sick.**	**We will get sick.**
I will die.	**You will die.**	**We will die.**

You are reciting the three judgments that are rendered to all living beings.

You may find this exercise difficult to practice at first. In time, you may find, in ways that surprise you, that bringing awareness to such deep truths that unite us all can be a powerful force that frees you from unpleasant thoughts and feelings.

You become more productive, less thrown off by the conduct of another, and experience a greater sense of well-being.

The 10-Minute Body Scan

Preliminary Instructions:

Wear comfortable clothes and take off your shoes. Lay on your back, arms resting by your side. Consider putting a pillow under your knees to avoid strain on your lower back. Don't worry about doing this exercise "right." This is one big "right" brain activity. What's important is that you are doing it.

Instructions:

1. Close your eyes and bring awareness to your breathing.
2. Direct attention to your left foot.
3. As you breathe in, slowly scan your left leg from toes to your thigh. As you breathe out, reverse the scan from thigh to toes. Rest awareness on this part of your body for a few breaths. Note any sensations. Pay attention to how they arise and change. If thoughts appear, as they will throughout this exercise, that's fine. Treat them as just another sensation. Gently bring awareness back to your breath.
4. Move awareness to your right foot.
5. As you breathe in, slowly scan your right leg from toes to knee, and up through your thigh. As you breathe out, reverse the scan from thigh to toes. Rest awareness on this part of your body for a few breaths, noting any sensations. Now bring awareness to your groin, hips, genitals, and buttocks, and allow it to rest there as you note sensations.
6. Move awareness to your stomach. Feel it rising as you breathe in, sinking as you exhale. Sense this movement, aware of sensations.
7. Direct your awareness to your left hand. Scan along the length of your left arm, and across your chest then down your right arm to your right hand. Breathe and observe.
8. Bring awareness to your chest and rest awareness on your lungs, heart, and back. Hold awareness in this part of your body and notice what sensations arise.
9. Continue scanning up along your neck and to your face. Feel any sensations in your throat, your jaw, your nose, sinuses, eyes and ears, your skull. Breathe.
10. Sense your entire body, from the top of your head to the tips of your toes. Observe any sensations. Notice how they arise, change, and fall away.
11. Rest in awareness for a few moments as you conclude this exercise. When you are ready, sit up slowly.

Resources

Books

Kabat-Zinn, J., *Full Catastrophe Living: Using the Wisdom of your Body and Mind to Face Stress, Pain and Illness* (Delta 1990).

Lewis, D., *Free Your Breath, Free Your Life* (Shambhala, 2004).

Ricard, M., *Happiness* (Little Brown, 2006).

Articles

Carey B., "Lotus Therapy," *New York Times* (May 27, 2008).

Riskin, L., "Awareness in Lawyering: A Primer on Paying Attention," in *The Affective Assistance of Counsel: Practicing Law as a Healing Profession* 447—71 (Marjorie Silver, ed., Carolina Academic Press, 2007).

Rogers, S. "Harnessing the Hand Dial: Cultivating Mindful Awareness amid Interpersonal Challenge—An Interpersonal Neurobiology Application of Dan Siegel's 'Wheel of Awareness.'" Presented at the Mindsight Institute, August 2, 2008.

Websites

The Mindful Law Student, www.themindfullawstudent.com/learnedhand.html

CHAPTER 10

Going Through the Motions

Legal motions and court orders are the lifeblood of the legal system. In *Jurisight*, they offer you an opportunity to examine more closely the activity of your mind and consider how you might optimize your experience. The *Motion for Relief from Judgment* asks you to consider the toll taken by a mind that continually generates evaluations, comparisons, and judgments that may not always serve your best interests. The *Motion to Recuse* asks the paradoxical question of who would be making your decisions, if not your judging mind. The mindfulness teachings on relating to distracting and unpleasant thoughts and feelings is examined in the *Motion to Quash*. Lastly, you'll find the *Motion to Embrace Uncertainty* to offer both a mindfulness route to relating to the uncertainties inherent in the law school experience, as well as a mindfulness cue you can use to help you reclaim present-moment awareness when circumstances have led your mind astray and rattled your body. While the mindfulness cue appears as an Exhibit affixed to the Motion, you can contact the Institute for Mindfulness Studies and a real one will be sent to you.

As you'll notice, some of the Motions are accompanied by Orders. Mindfulness involves attention to your intention. It is one thing to read something and agree with its content. It's another to engage the intentional network in your mind that transforms the experience. As you rule on these motions, do so with an intentionality of mind and heart that not only offers you a taste of this moment, but also a glimpse of your extraordinary nature.

Other Motions not included in this book but which can be found on The Mindful Law Student Website include:

Motion for Clarification (of Judgments)
Motion to Bifurcate (Pain and Suffering)
Motion to Withdraw (from Life's Trials and Tribulations)
Motion to Supplement (Witness List)
Motion for Joinder (of all Beings)
Motion to Dissolve (Self)

IN THE NEURAL CIRCUIT COURT IN AND FOR THE GREAT AND HEALTHY STATE OF MIND

YOU, aka "ME"

                Petitioner,

        vs.

REALITY

                Respondent.

_____/

MOTION FOR RELIEF FROM JUDGMENT

Pursuant to the laws of the great and healthy State of Mind, Petitioner respectfully moves for relief from the unnecessary pain and suffering caused by the never-ending judgments that arise in the mind.

1. Petitioner has been blessed with an intellect and capacity to reason, analyze, judge, and make decisions.

2. Much of Petitioner's prior experience has positively reinforced these skills, especially the ability to make judgments about facts, events, other persons, and Petitioner.

3. Petitioner has survived all prior obstacles and challenges and unconsciously attributes this survival to a panoply of skills, especially the making of judgments. This attribution is in and of itself a judgment.

4. Due to the enormous volume of judgments generated by Petitioner's mind, coupled with there having been positive reinforcement by virtue of Petitioner's survival, it has become impossible to efficiently discern judgments based on law and fact and admitted as credible evidence from those not based on law and fact, or that constitute hearsay.

5. As a result, the incessant flow of judgments has led to circumstances where Petitioner overreacts to circumstances; prejudges; misjudges; criticizes people and events; and interacts with people and treats oneself in a manner that is biased and based on erroneous assumptions —all of which causes undue pain and suffering.

WHEREFORE, Petitioner seeks relief from the unnecessary pain and suffering occasioned by this always-judging nature.

                Respectfully submitted,

                _____

                YOU, Esq.
                Counsel for Petitioner

The Motion for Relief from Judgment is a reminder of the many ways your mind effortlessly generates judgment after judgment and how this tendency can bring about unnecessary pain and suffering.

On a separate piece of paper write down three names: a person with whom you have a close relationship, a person whom you do not care for, and your name. Place one near the top, one in the middle and one toward the bottom of the page.

In the space below each name, write down your general sense of the person—their strengths and their weaknesses. Write down as many characteristics as come to mind in a few minutes.

Place a plus sign by those that are positive and a minus sign by those that are negative.

For each person, look over the critical judgments that have a minus sign by them. How do you feel when you consider these items?

Then, look over the positive items and do the same.

You have been generating and refining many of these judgments for a long time. You probably never gave yourself the task of doing so. It simply is something your mind does.

Can you tap into the source of these judgments?

What is their purpose?

How certain are you that they are accurate?

When you are ready, reread the Motion and consider how you would rule.

Would you enter the Order on the following page?

IN THE NEURAL CIRCUIT COURT IN AND FOR THE GREAT AND HEALTHY STATE OF MIND

YOU, aka "ME"

                     Petitioner,

        vs.

REALITY

                     Respondent.

_____/

ORDER GRANTING RELIEF FROM JUDGMENT

Before this Neural Circuit Court is Petitioner's Motion for Relief from Judgment. For the reasons set forth below, Petitioner's Motion is GRANTED.

1. This Court finds that Petitioner is continually making judgments about everything that arises in Petitioner's mind.

2. This Court also finds that the enormous quantity of thoughts and feelings continuously arising in Petitioner's mind, along with Petitioner's prior conditioning, makes it humanly impossible to efficiently discern judgments based on facts admitted into evidence from those not in evidence.

3. This Court also finds that as a result, Petitioner will, from time to time and often without awareness, overreact to circumstances; prejudge people and outcomes; and interact with people and treat oneself in a manner that is biased and based on erroneous assumptions—all of which is likely to cause undue pain and suffering.

ACCORDINGLY, Petitioner's Motion for Relief from Judgment is GRANTED. This Order will be SELF-enforcing. Although this Court, being a Neural Circuit Court, is mindful of the challenges (and paradox) inherent in looking to the self to enforce this order, it believes that such collaboration is necessary in order to ensure the long-term relief that is sought.

Done and ordered in Chambers this ____ day of _____.

                             _____

                             The Honorable You
                             Neural Circuit Court Judge

IN THE NEURAL CIRCUIT COURT IN AND FOR
THE GREAT AND HEALTHY STATE OF MIND

YOU, aka "ME"

                  Petitioner,

    vs.

REALITY

                  Respondent.

_____/

MOTION TO QUASH

Pursuant to the laws of the great and healthy State of Mind, Petitioner respectfully moves for an order quashing all thoughts that cause unnecessary pain and suffering.

1. Petitioner's brain is a thinking machine. One of its primary functions is to continuously generate thoughts and feelings.

2. Petitioner's brain generates thoughts 24/7. The State Bar will not allow Petitioner to bill for this time when Petitioner begins practicing law. However, Petitioner is continually paying for it.

3. Many of these thoughts are neither productive nor constructive. They tend to focus on past events for which there is regret and toward future events for which there is worry.

4. This tendency to dwell in the past and anticipate the future has, over time, become an almost natural state of affairs.

5. As a result, Petitioner is unable to experience the depth of well-being and clarity of mind that flows out of the present moment. Indeed, the quality of relationships with others and oneself, along with productivity at school and home, has been compromised.

WHEREFORE, Petitioner respectfully requests that this Court order that all thoughts causing unnecessary pain and suffering be quashed.

Respectfully submitted,

_____

YOU, Esq.
Counsel for Petitioner

The Motion to Quash makes explicit the pain and suffering associated with mental chatter and distraction and seeks to quash such mental activity.

From what you have learned thus far about mindfulness, do you think that eliminating these comparisons, evaluations, and judgments from the mind is the proper remedy?

After finishing this Motion, consider how you would rule.

Go online and read "The Guest House" by the poet Rumi. You will find it easily. What does this poem say to you about mindfulness and the unpleasant thoughts and feelings you experience from time to time?

After reflecting on this, would you enter the Order found on the following page?

IN THE NEURAL CIRCUIT COURT IN AND FOR THE GREAT AND HEALTHY STATE OF MIND

YOU, aka "ME"

                    Petitioner,

        vs.

REALITY

                    Respondent.

_____/

ORDER DENYING MOTION TO QUASH

Before this Neural Circuit Court is Petitioner's Motion to Quash all thoughts that cause unnecessary pain and suffering. For the reasons set forth below, Petitioner's Motion is DENIED.

1. This Court finds that Petitioner's brain is a thinking machine whose primary function is to continuously generate thoughts.

2. This Court also finds that many of these thoughts are neither productive nor constructive, and that they dwell on past events for which there is regret and toward future events for which there is worry. This tendency to dwell in the past and anticipate the future has, over time, become an almost natural state of affairs.

3. This Court also finds that Petitioner is unable to experience the depth of well-being or clarity of mind that flows out of the present moment, and that as a result, the quality of relationships with others and oneself, along with productivity at school and home have been compromised.

4. This Court, however, being a specialized Neural Circuit Court, does not judge the thoughts that arise in the mind. It finds, as a matter natural law, that all thoughts may be welcomed, allowed to arise and pass away in their own due time.

Done and ordered in Chambers this ____ day of _____.

_____
Judge You
Neural Circuit Judge

IN THE NEURAL CIRCUIT COURT IN AND FOR
THE GREAT AND HEALTHY STATE OF MIND

YOU, aka "ME"

                  Petitioner,

       vs.

REALITY

                  Respondent.

_____/

MOTION TO RECUSE

Pursuant to the laws of the great and healthy State of Mind, Petitioner respectfully moves for the recusal of Petitioner **as judge** over these proceedings. For the reasons set forth below, Judge You should be recused from these proceedings.

1. <u>No Accountability:</u> Judge You was not elected, was not appointed, and was not even confirmed with the advice and consent of anyone.

2. <u>No Experience:</u> Judge You had no prior experience. He didn't even have all of his brain cells when he took the bench.

3. <u>Conflict of Interest:</u> Judge You has multiple conflicts of interest. These include, *inter alia:*

   a. He has a personal bias against the Respondent, Reality, when it does not go his way.
   b. He has been known to deny Reality without giving it an opportunity to be heard.

4. <u>Lack of Jurisidiction:</u> Notwithstanding that the jurisdictional limits of Judge You's authority is his own life, he continues to judge everybody else's life.

5. <u>Ex Parte Communications:</u> Judge You continues to engage in ex parte communications with himself. Judge You is constantly issuing Temporary Restraining Orders seeking to maintain the status quo.

6. <u>Improper Use of Interpreter:</u> When the Court has required the use of an interpreter to clarify and explain past events, Judge You has appointed himself to serve as interpreter and provided a biased and partial interpretation of events and witnesses statements.

7. <u>Prejudgment of Facts and Law:</u> Judge You has a need to be right and for others to be wrong. In addition, he prejudges facts, witnesses, and the law. Judge You has his own preferences for the laws of nature and, when Reality does not go his way, he becomes angry, frustrated, and resists accepting it. On occasions, Judge You is so resistant to reality that he is afraid to rule on pending motions and, as a result, has an overwhelming docket.

8. <u>Double Bias:</u> The only argument advanced in opposition to recusal is that Judge You is often harsh, judgmental, doubtful, and critical of himself. This, too, however, supports a finding of bias. Clearly, this is not a judge who has a balanced and even judicial temperament over matters involving his life, liberty, or pursuit of happiness.

WHEREFORE, for the reasons set forth above, the **Motion to Rescue** (sic) should be granted.

Respectfully submitted,

_____

You, Esq.
Counsel for Petitioner

This motion is a reminder of the many ways your mind is continually comparing, evaluating, and judging your experience.

After reading this motion, consider how you would rule.

Consider how your life would be different if you embraced a nonjudging orientation.

What might be lost? How would that make you feel?

What might be gained? How would you feel about that?

This is one of those motions that you get to take under advisement. But do return to it from time to time.

IN THE NEURAL CIRCUIT COURT IN AND FOR
THE GREAT AND HEALTHY STATE OF MIND

YOU, aka "ME"

Petitioner,

vs.

REALITY

Respondent.

_____/

MOTION TO EMBRACE LIFE'S UNCERTAINTIES

Pursuant to the laws of the great and healthy State of Mind, Petitioner respectfully moves this neural circuit court for *relief from judgment* so that Petitioner may embrace life's uncertainties with optimism and courage.

1. Judging the Future: In an effort to survive, an overzealous "Me" will occasionally prejudge the future. These judgments are almost always fear-based, and as such, anticipate worst-case scenarios that become a source of anxiety and worry.

2. The Wandering Mind: As these judgments about the future proliferate, thinking becomes scattered and it is difficult to stay on track and attend to work, family, and friends with focus, clarity, and compassion.

3. The Afflicted Body: This mental activity takes its toll on the brain and body as memory becomes impaired, the cardiovascular system is taxed, and immune functioning deteriorates.

4. Mindfulness: Psychologists and neuroscientists are finding that "uncertainty" is not the source of alarm, but rather, how Petitioner relates to uncertainty. Mindfulness invites Petitioner to move toward the discomfort by embracing life's forever-uncertain nature.

5. Neuroscience: Neuroscientists and psychologists are finding that by embracing the discomfort that arises amid life's uncertainties, mind and body move into greater balance and integration.

6. Practice: Petitioner can embrace life's uncertainties with optimism and courage by:

   a. Placing the Tee, attached as Exhibit "A," in plain view on their desk.

114

b. During challenging moments of uncertainty, allowing the Tee to serve as a reminder that worrisome thoughts and feelings are momentary activities of the mind and body that arise and pass away.

c. Slowly reaching out a hand and embracing the "Uncertain-Tee," as a reminder that the discomfort is bearable.

d. "Seeing" the color of the Tee, "feeling" its texture, and exploring other sensory experiences like sound, taste, and smell, thereby quieting the mind.

e. Breathing. Bringing awareness to your beating heart. Smiling.

WHEREFORE, for the reasons set forth above, the Motion to Embrace should be granted.

Respectfully submitted,

_____

YOU, Esq.
Counsel for Petitioner

This motion is a reminder that it is through your willingness to move into uncomfortable and unfamiliar territory of the mind that you can move beyond fear.

You can use any Tee as a mindfulness cue or reminder. Send an e-mail to the Institute for Mindfulness Studies requesting a Tee and a red Uncertain-Tee will be sent to you.

As you read the motion, can you think of a reason to not grant it?

Turn the page and examine the illustration.

Can you relate to the trials and tribulations of the Tee?

What is the lesson of the last panel on the bottom right?

Some of Life's Uncertain-Tees™

"Selfdoubt"

"Things not working out as planned"

"People getting upset or disapproving"

"Rejection"

"Fear"

"Will it ever end?"

Illustration 10.1

Glossary of Brain Imaging Technologies

CT: Computed tomography machine (also CAT) uses an X-ray that revolves around the head, generating images of various slices of the brain.

EEG: Electroencephalography uses electrodes placed on the scalp to detect and measure patterns of electrical activity emanating from the brain. EEG records patterns of neural activity occurring within fractions of a second after a stimulus has been administered.

MEG: Magnetoencephalography measures the magnetic fields produced by electrical activity in the brain via very sensitive devices. It offers a direct measurement of neural electrical activity.

MRI: Magnetic resonance imaging uses magnetic fields and radio waves to produce high-quality, two- or three-dimensional images of brain structures without the use of X-rays or radioactive tracers.

fMRI: Functional magnetic resonance imaging relies on the properties of oxygenated and deoxygenated hemoglobin to see images of changing blood flow in the brain associated with neural activity. This allows images to be generated that reflect which brain structures are activated (by measuring blood flow) during the performance of different tasks.

PET: Positron emission tomography measures emissions from radioactively labeled chemicals that have been injected into the bloodstream where they collect in active areas of the brain. The radioactivity helps map brain activity from moment to moment.

SPECT: Single photon emission computed tomography uses gamma ray–emitting radioisotopes and a gamma camera to record data that a computer uses to construct two- or three-dimensional images of active brain regions.

TMS: Transcranial magnetic stimulation is a noninvasive method using a coil of wire that sends a brief magnetic pulse to excite neurons in the brain. Scientists are able to infer the function of neurons just beneath the coil.

About the Author

Scott Rogers, MS, JD, is founder and director of the Institute for Mindfulness Studies. He has practiced law for 17 years and mindfulness and other contemplative practices for more than 16 years. His concentration on mindfulness is rooted in his belief that it offers the most effective means of introducing a contemplative practice to attorneys and law students, and to encourage meaningful inner work and growth, both professionally and personally. In 2003, Scott began developing Jurisight®, the mindfulness-based program designed for lawyers and law students.

Scott received his master's degree in social psychology and his law degree from the University of Florida, graduating summa cum laude. He has chaired the Education Subcommittee of the Dade County Bar Association's Professionalism Committee and speaks with law students and lawyers about the mindful practice of law. Scott served as a judicial law clerk to federal and state court judges at the federal district, federal appellate, and the state supreme court levels. He practiced commercial litigation at White & Case LLP, appeared before state and federal courts, and served as general counsel and president to an Internet company. The breadth of Scott's experience across diverse areas of the law allows him to relate to the work and experiences of law students, beginning and seasoned lawyers, educators, and jurists.

Scott has appeared on television and National Public Radio, been interviewed for newspapers and magazines, and speaks across the country to law students, lawyers, mediators, and experts in conflict resolution. He has presented his work to numerous professional groups interested in neuroscience and mindfulness practices.

Scott lives in Miami Beach, Florida, with his wife and two children.

About the Illustrator

Cathy Gibbs Thornton is a graphic designer and illustrator with over 28 years' experience in the creative, advertising, and printing industries. Originally from Barbados, Cathy studied art in the United States, where she received an associate degree from International Fine Arts College, and a bachelor of arts degree in Advertising Communications from The Union Institute, graduating summa cum laude both times. She worked as a senior designer and art/creative director for large advertising agencies in Barbados and in Miami before opening her own business, CG Graphics.

Over the years, Cathy's award-winning artwork has been featured in several publications, including the *Miami Herald* and the cover of *South Florida* magazine. Cathy takes pride in working closely with her clients in the United States, Canada, and throughout the Caribbean region, helping them achieve their creative goals. Her illustrations encompass both traditional and digital media, and her design capabilities include both two- and three-dimensional designs. She specializes in logo, brochure, and ad design. Local examples of her work in the Miami area include the official logos for the Village of Palmetto Bay and the Town of Cutler Bay, both award-winning competition entries.

Cathy lives in Miami, Florida, with her husband Mike, daughter Natasha, and son Jason.

Institute for Mindfulness Studies

Founded in 2004, the Institute for Mindfulness Studies is dedicated to the transformation of the practice of law, and the legal system, from one that creates unnecessary pain and suffering for its participants into one that fulfills its original mandate of contributing to a more peaceful society through a process of collaboration, wisdom, integrity, and professionalism.

The Institute for Mindfulness Studies developed Jurisight® to introduce mindfulness practices to law students, law professors, lawyers, paralegals, judges, and legislators. This transformation will take place through the integration of mindfulness principles and insights into the landscape of the law, and the minds and hearts of its students and practitioners.

One aspiration of Jurisight® is that participants in the legal system will share a vocabulary, an understanding of the nature of mind, and the ability to respond to events and encourage others to respond to events from states of greater mindful awareness of what is actually taking place in the present moment.

The Institute for Mindfulness Studies offers presentations and workshops to law schools, to small and large law firms, and to organizations that employ lawyers.

MINDFULLIVING.NET

Mindfulliving.net is the umbrella website for the Institute for Mindfulness Studies. Websites devoted specifically to legal professionals include:

TheMindfulLawyer.com
TheMindfulLawStudent.com
TheMindfulLawProfessor.com
Jurisight.com

You may contact us by e-mail at contact@mindfulliving.net, or by writing us at:

Institute for Mindfulness Studies, Inc.
800 West Avenue, Suite C-1
Miami Beach, FL 33139

CPSIA information can be obtained
at www.ICGtesting.com
Printed in the USA
FSOW02n1429220816
24057FS